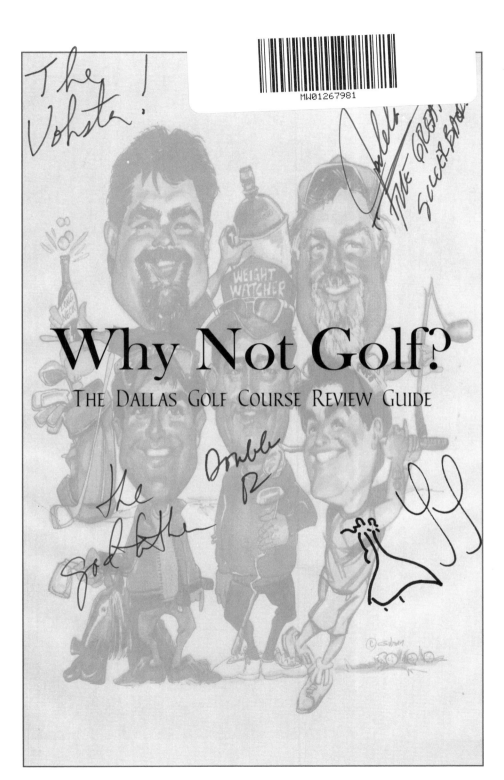

Why Not Golf?

The Dallas Golf Course Review Guide

Why Not Golf?

THE DALLAS GOLF COURSE REVIEW GUIDE

"The Goofy Golfers"

With Lynn McWilliams

Fore!
Lyn

ZONE PRESS
Denton, Texas

Why Not Golf?
The Dallas Golf Course Review

Zone Press
an imprint of Rogers Publishing and Consulting, Inc.
109 East Oak – Suite 300
Denton, Texas 76201
info@zonepress.com

Jim O. Rogers - Editor
Charlotte Beckham - Copy Edit
Lori Walker - Production and Design
Jim O. Rogers - Cover Design
Jenny Morlan - Graphic Art

All art and photographic images used in this publication were utilized with written permision from:
Mary Gibson, Artist
Robert McCullough, Photographer
Dee Thomas, Photographer

Printed in the United States of America
ISBN:0-9761706-4-7

Why Not Golf?
Contents

Dedication -	7
Special Thanks -	8
Acknowledgements -	9
Foreward -	11
Meet The Goofy Golfers -	13
Evaluation System -	25
Best Overall Top 20 -	29
Cowboys Golf Club -	30
The Tribute Golf Links -	32
Tour 18 -	34
Bear Creek Golf Club -	36
Indian Creek Golf Club -	38
Woodbridge Golf Club -	40
Lantana Golf Club -	42
Twin Lakes Golf Course -	44
The Heritage Ranch Golf and Country Club -	46
Garden Valley Golf Club-	48
Chase Oaks Golf Club -	50
The Links At Lands End -	52
Tierra Verde Golf Club -	54
Buffalo Creek Golf Club -	56
Tenison Park Golf Course -	58
Pine Dunes Resort and Golf Club -	60
The Golf Club at KcKinney -	62
Westridge Golf Course -	64
Bridlewood Golf Club -	66
The Golf Club at Castle Hills -	68
AAKI Ranch International Golf Course -	72
Cedar Crest Golf Course -	74
C. W. Ditto Golf Course -	76
Country View Golf Club -	78
Coyote Ridge Golf Club -	80

Creekview Golf Club - 82

Eagle Rock Golf Club (Formerly The Summit) - 84

Firewheel Golf Park - 86

Grapevine Golf Course - 90

Keeton Park Golf Course - 92

Lake Arlington Golf Course - 94

Lake Park Golf Club - 96

L. B. Houston Park Golf Course - 98

Legacy Ridge Country Club - 100

Los Rios Country Club - 102

Mesquite Golf Course - 104

Oak Hollow Golf Course - 106

Old Brickyard Golf Course - 108

Pecan Hollow Golf Course - 110

Plantation Golf Club - 112

Prairie Lakes Golf Course - 114

Red Oak Valley Golf Club - 116

Ridgeview Ranch Golf Club - 118

Riverchase Golf Club - 120

Riverside Golf Club - 122

Sherrill Park Golf Course - 124

Stevens Park Golf Course - 126

Tangle Ridge Golf Club - 128

The Golf Club of Twin Creeks - 130

The Pinnacle Club - 132

The Shores Country Club - 134

Twin Wells Golf Course - 136

Waterview Golf Club - 138

Webb Hill Country Club - 140

Best Overall Top 20 - 143

Top Municipal Courses - 147

Best/Worst Game - 151

Rankings - 155

Fantasy Golf Course - 163

Frequently Asked Questions - 171

Glossary - 177

Map of Golf Course Locations - 188

Dedication

You don't go from five average guys playing golf to publishing a serious golf course review book without signficant help. Therefore, we have a lot of people who deserve special recognition.

First of all, we would like to thank God for opening so many doors and giving us unbelievable opportunities beyond our wildest dreams.

To Steven Gribin, ESPN 103.3 FM, who included us in his radio show every Sunday morning for the last few years. His trust took our unique perspective of golf to a much broader audience and clearly lifted us out of the water hazard and into the fairway. Thanks for everything Gribby.

To Lynn McWilliams for keeping us focused and headed in the right direction. Thanks for your patience, tolerance, guidance and careful way with words. You accurately recognized and harnessed our talents. We *really* couldn't have done it without you.

To Lori Barber-Thomas and Net Success, whose vision took us beyond our golf carts and into cyberspace. Her encouragement and support continuously keeps us going forward.

To our 'secretary' Cheryl Zmolik, who helped out on countless business details with no pay and only The Vokster for solace.

To Mom and Dad Zmolik, thanks for being our original and most ardent fans, even though Dad could not care less about 'cow pasture pool'.

To Mom and Dad Rodgers, for their loyal support and for providing a lifetime free parking spot for our antique RV, even though it does help hide their yacht.

To Aunt Carolyn and Luke's sisters who have always been there when we needed them. And to Luke's Dad who is smiling or shaking his head, or both, from heaven.

To Grandma Marsha James, thank you for all your help, especially with the kids.

To all the children, ex-wives, future ex-wives, babysitters, family and friends who were an integral part of this book by donating their time, support and encouragement.

Special thanks to all the golf courses in the metroplex who have welcomed us with open arms and recognized that we are an asset to the industry.

And lastly, but certainly not least, much gratitude to all the other golfers out there who have told us their stories, shared their tips, appreciated our knickers and bought this book!

We have met some incredible people and loved every minute of it.

The Goofy Golfers

Special Thanks

To my husband, Keith, who has never stopped believing, loving and encouraging me.

For my sister, Roni 'Willis' Milligan, who always gives me staying power and a fresh perspective.

For Lori and Steven Lacore, whose safe and loving care for Benjamin provides precious peace of mind for his parents.

For my mother, Betty Carroll Whitley, who always said I could do anything I put my mind to.

For the trust of five crazy golfers despite long hours and wildly different points of view.

And especially for Ben, who makes me thankful for my blessings, tickles me, renews my imagination and shows me the future *every single day*.

I could not have done it without you and I love you all,

Lynn McWilliams

Acknowledgements

Mary Gibson is a talented artist from Honey Grove, Texas, whose caricatures of The Goofy Golfers have helped to make their unique personalities come to life.
Contact information for Mary: 214-354-8704.

Robert McCullough, a Pulitzer Nominee from Flower Mound,Texas, shot Lynn McWilliams' portrait image and images used to develop the book cover.
Contact information for Robert: 3105 Springwood Rd, Flower Mound, Texas 75028

Dee Thomas, a portrait and Special Events photographer shot the portrait images of The Goofy Golfers.
Contact information for Dee: 214-697-8094

Cover images were shot on the number four hole at
The Cowboys Golf Club
1600 Fairway Drive,
Grapevine, Texas 76051
817/481-7277

Foreword

Almost three years ago, I met five of the strangest fellows imaginable. They wore old shoes, weird pants and drove around in the ugliest RV on this planet. But, all had one thing in common, an incredible love for the game of golf. In fact, their passion for golf was so contagious, I quickly invited them to be guests on my radio show. The audience enjoyed their stories so much, that soon, 'The Goofy Golfers' became regulars on Sunday Tee Time.

Best of all, they review golf courses for you and me, not the lucky guy who can get on any course he wants. They have actually played them too, from the smallest 'wanna-be' municipal to the top-notch public course everyone dreams about playing. Their insights in this book provide a much needed average mans' look at all the golfing in the Dallas area.

There are many books about golf covering everything from what to do, to where to go. Some are filled with too much information and others come under the heading of 'fluff'. This one falls exactly in the center and will give you all the information you need while making you laugh at the same time.

Some of the best courses in the nation are located in the Dallas/Fort Worth area. So, it makes perfect sense that an easy guide about where to go based on your experience, handicap, strengths and weaknesses would be a must have. It is also good to be reminded that on your worst day, someone else is out there playing from the rough, too!

The Goofy Golfers are what this sport is all about: passion, truth, sharing time with your friends, perhaps a good (or cheap) beer and mostly, love of the greatest sport on earth. I love The Goofy Golfers and all they stand for.....and I believe you will, too.

Steve Gribin
Sunday Tee Time
ESPN 103.3 FM, 7 – 9 a.m.

Meet The Goofy Golfers

The Control Freak

The Godfather
Handicap 10.45

Ahhhh! The Godfather…. The youngest and most powerful one of the crew, 'The Godfather' is the driving force behind The Goofy Golfers. Named 'The Godfather' because of his love of the movie, he says he feels like the character Al Pacino made famous and acknowledges a need to be totally in control of everything around him. Rumor has it his nieces and nephews kiss his ring, just to perpetuate the myth.

Youngest of the five Zmolik boys, he is nevertheless the person who delegates all the work out. According to him, "Someone has to do it!" Michael is a single dad with three children, ages 18, 15, and 13. He says the 'labor of love' keeps him constantly on task and at full throttle. In fact, Michael is the one who doled out the nicknames for The Goofy Golfers, using his unique position in the family to size up and figure them all out. He knows as the youngest in the group, that respect for the others is a valuable key and works hard to both give and earn it. Actually, the jokes on him, they just want him to take charge so they don't have to!

The Godfather believes his mental game on the golf course is most important and gives him a decided edge. One of the better golfers of the group, he is not bothered by the clutch shots, stays on focus and gets the job done. His greatest challenge is controlling Jodella! Usually partnered up together, he finds himself trying to tame the ever impatient Great Silverback and constantly reminds him to keep his language under check. Hysterical to watch, these two in a golf cart are reminiscent of comedy days gone by. Jodella drives at a full boar pace and stops with equal force. Michael is thrown about like a rag doll, while trying to secure the beers and calm down his frustrated partner, making the game hardly relaxing!

Short irons are the worst part of the game for 'The Godfather'. While he is consistent on his drives and good at staying in the fairways, his short irons cost him a lot of strokes. His chipping and putting are very good, but definitely those short irons could use some extra work.

'The Godfather' is a man of his word. Despite his moniker, he is not arrogant and serves as a wonderful friend to everyone. He looks up to his brothers and knows they would do anything for him. By his own admission, he is an extreme future thinker and very goal oriented.

Michael is part owner of a custom homes company. Clearly a lady killer, he is known for his ability to consider women's opinions and make them feel good. Passionate, fun loving and dedicated to a natural high on life, you can bet he will never lie and always has his priorities in order. What's not to love? Well, the man has a reputation for machine gun profanity on the course. But hey, being the perfectionist he is, you can bet he's working on that, too!

The Consummate Planner

Double R
Handicap 9.91

The quietest Goofy Golfer is definitely "Double R". So named from his 'RR' initials, Riley Rodgers likes things simple: black and white. Never one to fly off the handle, he is known to think before he says anything and even leans toward being a little too logical.

'Double R' believes his best golf trait is patience on the course. He doesn't let the others interfere with his game (imagine that!) and is known for his stellar concentration. He never counts himself the loser until the last hole, when it is obvious what the outcome will be.

But don't misunderstand; Riley does not like to lose. He will play any game for fun, as long as you realize that if he plays, he is going to try to beat you. And when he does win, most often he will be heard to say, 'I just got lucky', though secretly he knows better.

Putting is the curse 'Double R' is experiencing lately. He used to be great at it, but now he is horrible and doesn't really know why. On the outside, he may appear cool, but inside he will be beating himself up over mistakes and planning to throw that putter off the nearest bridge on the way home.

Riley worked in Management for Minyards until about 10 years ago, when the Zmolik brothers offered him a job as a residential homebuilder superintendent. After 25 years in food retail, he counts himself lucky to enjoy going to work. Back at the ranch, he is recently divorced after

29 years of marriage. He is the father of 3 grown boys and 2 incredible grandsons.

Double R says golf has always been a way for him to escape and most times, even when he's not playing, he's thinking about it. Handsome in his knickers, Riley brings polish and shine to The Goofy Golfers and is the calm spot in their calamity. He loves to laugh and can raise a few toasts with the best of them, but underneath it all, you can be sure he's already planning a winning strategy for the next golf game.

Gale Force Winds

Jodella
Handicap 14.56

Jodella insures that The Goofy Golfers will never be a boring group. Quick to respond to everything, he is a highly organized ball of fire with a big heart, who is very opinionated. Trouble is, he's perpetually on a very short fuse.

It is no surprise that Jodella has a temper. What's funny is that he believes he has learned to control it! Hanging with Jodella is a roller coaster ride that can erupt in profanity one minute and tenderness the next. More outspoken than possibly any person on the planet, even when he tries to whisper, it is incredibly loud.

But the vortex of the tornado reveals a person who has many talents. Married 18 years to Lisa, they have five children. As the oldest of nine children himself, Jodella excels at entertaining them all with a lovable, silly side that might surprise a bystander. Those who take the time to know him are also treated to a very giving person, who in fact, is bothered when people don't like him. And his employees have learned that even when the temper erupts, 15 minutes later there will be an apology along with a little extra in their paycheck for 'ass chewing compensation'.

In the group, Jodella is the one who is the most likely to get pissed off first. Like all The Goofy Golfers, Jodella always plays from the tips and his biggest challenge is patience. By his own admission, he has 'invisible gun powder spewing from his ass and it only takes one spark to ignite it'. Luckily, it never lasts more than five minutes and besides, he is much better than he used to be! The Great Silverback's strong point is putting, but just hitting short irons is really what he does best. Of course, his biggest problem is inconsistency, so that sort of evens the whole thing out. Hands down, he can hit the ball farther than anyone, but growls when he has to admit that he 'doesn't know where in the hell it will go'!

Jodella played varsity football in high school and actually marvels that no one wanted to go up against him. A supervisor and wood framer in real life, he is quick to point out that he is a damn good businessman and very competitive in his field.

If you read 'The Godfathers' profile, you know Jodella does not play golf for the serenity of it. But he does say that golf is a game for life, because it teaches you so much. Claiming it humbles, rewards and provides constant adventure; he thoroughly enjoys the challenge it brings.

Jodella has thrown clubs and one time even broke two on one hole. He is absolutely larger than life and can blow hard enough to rattle the calmest golfing oasis. But that's the beauty of him, because in what is commonly known as one of the most frustrating games on record, who hasn't wanted to scream and rail against the gods of hooks and sand traps? And after all, he would be the first to tell you that just because he's loud, doesn't mean he's not a kind and understanding guy. So there.

Luke, The Fifth

Little Leonard
Handicap 10.69

Luke Zmolik, is the favorite cousin of the brothers Zmolik. No small accomplishment when you consider there are over 60 to choose from! Easily the most time challenged of the group, this divorced father of ten-year old twin boys, divides his time between their home in Virginia and his home in Plano, Texas. An equal parent in their lives, naturally the boys come first, followed closely by his high tech work as the developer of software designed to enhance the construction and framing process for builders (www.zlinksystems.com).

While Luke does share a deep love of golf with the other four, he is not always able to make the various tee times or scheduled events. Therefore, he is best known as the ever elusive 'fifth' Goofy Golfer, filling in whenever his real life juggling permits. Once on the course, his challenges change to keeping The Godfather out of his beer, staying consistent and trying to put two 9's together, but he loves it.

The only boy in a household of five, Luke knows about women and how they think. Growing up in Ennis, he was taught a deep appreciation for the fairer sex and could, but prefers not to, give advice to the others. However, he outshines them all in courtesy, kindness and just plain old-fashioned Texas charm. Affectionately named 'Little Leonard' and teased without ceasing for being the 'sheepherder' (you had to be there), he holds his own on the golf course with his subtle approach and determination to have fun.

What may surprise you about Little Leonard is his other hobby. He is also a very accomplished ballroom dancer and enjoys competing in that sport. It's a good thing he enjoys it so much, because you can rest assured he takes a ribbing about it from the other four Goofy Golfers! To his credit, he deals with them graciously. After all, at the end of the day he is still the only one who can Tango, Waltz, Foxtrot, Mambo and Samba with the ladies.

Little Leonard also has another leg up on the rest. Never one to sit around and enjoy idle time, about seven years ago he earned his Private Pilots license. Of course, one look at The Goofy Golfers and you know he would never fly that bunch anywhere. Can you imagine the chaos? Talk about air traffic control! No good day on the course is worth that kind of hassle. So instead, he is merely content to get to the course in the infamous RV, then 'sit back with Double R and just watch the show'.

Admittedly, catching a glimpse of Luke can be difficult. But when he does manage to make it, you can bet he will live up to the example set by his favorite golfer, Payne Stewart. He will be a man who has pizzazz, appreciation for the great outdoors, cuts a stylish swath and will keep his heart firmly in the game.

Got a Cold Beer?

The Vokster
Handicap 14.14

If there is a lovable teddy bear in the bunch, it would have to be The Vokster. Always up for a good time and ready to dispense a quip or quote to maintain the levity, The Vokster is the member who truly brings the word 'party' to the course. Number 2 in a family of nine full blooded Czechoslovakians, Wes could always be counted on to kick back and let the good times roll. The Godfather named him 'The Vokster' because his name in Czech is 'Voklov'. But he doesn't care what you call him as long as you order him another beer.

Ten years before The Goofy Golfers began their quest to bring golf to the average guy, he and Double R became good friends when their kids were playing football in high school. So naturally when the guys needed a 4th for golf, Wes suggested Riley fill the spot. Funny, true, trustworthy, easy to talk to and loaded with wisecracks, Wes just wants to keep the fun coming. Married to Cheryl for 17 years, together they have 5 children and 6 grandchildren.

The Vokster says his best golf trait (besides drinking) is accuracy. He doesn't hit the ball a long way, but he does always hit it just where he wants it to go. Conversely, that same strength also hurts his game and he believes it is what holds him back the most. But it doesn't matter! He loves being outside in nature and says that sometimes when he is surrounded by all the trees and the course is well manicured, "Honest To God, It's just like you are in Heaven!".

The Vokster has what he calls a comfortable mental game or 'smart golf'. He believes there is a time to go for it and a time not to. He is not big on swing mechanics or picking apart the process, he just focuses on the pure pleasure of it.

In real life, Wes is a self-employed framing contractor and more often than not, he can be found on a ladder swinging a hammer along with his crew. Golf provides him an outlet to get away from the normal workweek, or what he calls 'the hell of it'.

Wes admits he is the worst golfer of the 4, but it is not keeping him up nights. And about the worst you will hear him say is, "Why did that guy in Scotland pick up a stick and hit a rock anyway?" Why? Well, so Wes would have an excuse to order another cold beer.

Rare is the day that Wes beats the other three, but it does happen. And when it does, you can be sure he will say, "There's a new sheriff in town!" Okay, the star may be a little crooked and the reigns a little loose, but no matter, it will still be the biggest celebration in town!

The Evaluation System

Stars ☆ – Overall Grade

5 Stars – Excellent/Awesome
4 Stars – Very Good
3 Stars – Average
2 Stars – Fair
1 Star - Poor

Balls Practice Facility

5 Balls – Excellent
3 Balls – Average
1 Ball – Minimal

Cans ⬛ Bar/Beverage Rating

6 Pack – Awesome Bar/Beverage Cart
4 Cans – Average Bar/Beverage Cart
2 Cans – Small Bar/Minimal Cart Service
O Cans – No Liquor License

Dollars $ Cost of Play With Cart

$ - Up to $30.00
$$ - $31.00 to $60.00
$$$ - $61.00 to $100.00
$$$$ - $100 and up

Flags ⚑ Golf Course Grade

(Just the course nothing else)

5 Flags – Excellent/Awesome
4 Flags – Very Good
3 Flags – Average
2 Flags – Fair
1 Flag – Poor

Favorite Hole

Very challenging, scenic or fun to play

Reviews
Best Overall Top 20

Best Overall Top 20

Criteria: Layout, Challenge, Fun to Play, Customer Service, located in this designated area and if you are only playing 10-20 courses this year, play these.

1. **Cowboys Golf Club** – Best Overall
2. **The Tribute Golf Links** – Best Links Style
3. **Tour 18** – Best 18 Holes
4. **Bear Creek Golf Club** – Best Parkland Style
5. **Indian Creek Golf Club** – Best Municipal Course
6. **Woodbridge Golf Club** – Downright Toughest
7. **Lantana Golf Club** – Most Bunkers
8. **Twin Lakes Golf Course** – Best Value
9. **Heritage Ranch Golf and Country Club** – Favorite Par 3
10. **Garden Valley Golf Club** – Most Beautiful
11. **Chase Oaks Golf Club** – Most Water
12. **The Links At Lands End** – Favorite Lake Course
13. **Tierra Verde Golf Club** – Best Environmental Use
14. **Buffalo Creek Golf Club** – Best Mix of Holes
15. **Tenison Park Golf Course** (Tenison Highlands) – Best Redesign
16. **Pine Dunes Resort and Golf Club** – Best Towering Pines and Sand Combo
17. **The Golf Club At McKinney** – Toughest First Tee Shot
18. **Westridge Golf Course** – 6 par 3's, 6 Par 4's, 6 Par 5's on 18 holes
19. **Bridlewood Golf Club** – Best Subdivision Course
20. **The Golf Club At Castle Hills** – Demanding Par Fours

Cowboys Golf Club

This is the best golf course in Dallas. Jerry Jones, owner of the Dallas Cowboys, built this one of a kind course with an NFL Football theme and spared no expense. Conveniently located just on the edge of Grapevine and Flower Mound, this club is easily the premier daily fee course in the Dallas area. Range balls, food and non-alcoholic beverages are complimentary with your green fee. Best of all, the staff at Cowboys Golf Club cater to every golfer as if they were a member of a high end country club.

Most of the golf holes have some type of trouble on them, so the course will make you feel like a scared quarterback running from a blitzing defense. Visual stimulation from the tees include generous landing areas, tree lined holes and a huge blue star painted into the grass right in the middle of the #4 fairway. Take a moment to enjoy the view. This course is so well manicured, the attention to detail and definition of every aspect lends itself to the overall attraction.

Want more? Big multi-tiered greens with severe mounding brings a new dimension to putting. Well placed, steep faced bunkers create brutal lies. You're sure to find yourself a little awestruck. Where else is a putting green shaped like a star? This place is a golfer's dream come true.

The Godfather – Got a hard to buy for golfer? Let me recommend a sleeve of Titleist Pro V 1's, a Goofy Golfer cap and a gift certificate for a round of golf at Cowboy's Golf Club. Talk about scoring some serious points, that's always at the top of my list even if I have to buy it for myself.

Double R – When you think of the Dallas Cowboys, you think of winners. That is exactly what you have with the Cowboys Golf Club. After further review…. I demand an Instant Replay.

Jodella – Jerry Jones is not going to associate 'God's team' with just anything, image and ego are too important to him. You've got to play this course. I promise, you won't be disappointed. In fact, the only thing this course is missing are Dallas Cowboy Cheerleaders on the sidelines. Now THAT would significantly improve my game.

The Vokster – Two bits, four bits, six bits, a dollar. All for the Cowboys Golf Club stand up and swaller! Here's a toast to Jerry Jones, may he always have the money to keep the course in immaculate condition, may he consider adding alcoholic beverages to the list of freebies and may he put at least two season passes in my golf bag. Salute!

Cowboys Golf Club

	Par	Yardage	Rating	Slope
Black	72	7017	74.2	140
Silver	72	6563	71.7	130
White	72	5257	71.6	130
Gold	72	4702	68.9	114

1600 Fairway Drive
Grapevine, Texas 76051
(817) 481-7277

www.cowboysgolfclub.com

Greens – Tiff Eagle

Cost of Play – Mon-Thurs $$$$ Fri-Sun $$$$

Bar/Beverage Cart – 🛢 🛢 🛢 🛢 🛢 🛢

Practice Facility – ⬤ ⬤ ⬤ ⬤ ⬤

Course Grade – ⚑ ⚑ ⚑ ⚑ ⚑

Overall Grade – ☆ ☆ ☆ ☆ ☆

Favorite Hole – Hole #2, 376 Yards, Par 4

THE TRIBUTE GOLF LINKS

Scotland is the birthplace of golf. If you've ever wanted to play there, but could not, experience the next best thing right here in Texas! Located on the eastern shoreline of Lake Lewisville, The Tribute Golf Club has duplicated some of the most famous golf holes from Scotland, including Troon, Saint Andrews, and Prestwick. In fact, in keeping with true Scottish tradition, the flags are only 4 feet tall. So make sure you get a yardage guide and pin sheet before you begin.

A links style golf course at its finest, The Tribute comes complete with sawgrass covered dunes, wide undulating fairways and infamous pothole bunkers. You will very seldom have a level stance. If you have trouble hitting greens on other courses, you should not here. The greens are twice as large as most, so bad putters will struggle just to two putt.

To enjoy the experience to the fullest, caddies are available, just be sure to call in advance. With an outstanding clubhouse that looks like it was built in the 18th century, The Tribute also offers eight suites with stay and play packages in this new and oversized facility. Clearly a jewel in the crown of north Dallas courses, The Tribute is the Goofy Golfers #2 Best Overall Course To Play and holds the distinction of Best Links Style.

The Godfather – This golf course is way too easy. Am I the only genius in the metroplex that shoots my worse scores on wide-open golf courses? Definitely built to get as many golfers on and off the golf course as possible, my only mental game here should be trying to figure out how many times I can stop the beer cart. Unfortunately, all to often, I seem to find those pothole bunkers that require help from a buddy and a rope to get you out. I guess I need to rethink what I'm thinking about this "No Think" golf course.

Double R – If you have never played golf using a caddie, then you definitely need to play The Tribute. Their caddie program makes this great game even better and leaves me feeling like the pro that I'm not. If this is how they do it in Scotland, maybe I'll trade my knickers for a kilt.

Jodella – Make sure you bring a flashlight and compass when you play this course, so you can find your way out of the bunkers. It looks like the navy was using this course for target practice! If you find yourself in one of these bunkers, the only way to play out is backwards. But that's okay, my game's been going backwards for years anyway.

The Vokster – I'm glad somebody finally began using caddies. At last, I have some significant help with my beer cooler.

The Tribute Golf Links

	Par	Yardage	Rating	Slope
Yellow	72	7002	73.2	128
Black	72	6552	71.0	122
White	72	6002	68.9	116
Green	72	5352	65.6	111

1000 Boyd Road
The Colony, Texas 75056
(972) 370-5465

www.thetributegolflinks.com

Greens – Bent Grass

Cost of Play – Mon-Thurs $$$ Fri-Sun $$$

Bar/Beverage Cart –

Practice Facility – ⬤ ⬤ ⬤ ⬤ ⬤

Course Grade – 🚩 🚩 🚩 🚩 🚩

Overall Grade – ☆ ☆ ☆ ☆ ☆

Favorite Hole – Hole #17, 471 Yards, Par 4

TOUR 18

Nestled back off the beaten path among an exclusive enclave of beautiful homes, green fees are high at Tour 18, but well worth the price of admission. Every single hole has its' own unique style, so prepare to challenge your mind and set your boredom free.

Want to impress your friends? Take them to Tour 18. Considered America's greatest 18 holes of golf, you'll use every club in your bag to think your way around this course. One of only two such courses in the State of Texas, we are fortunate indeed to have this in our own back yard.

Test your PGA skills against such classic holes as Doral's #18, Sawgrass' #17, Riveria's #6 and the famous 'Amen Corner' trio from Augusta National. In fact, Tour 18 offers such euphoria; you will want to tee it up again as soon as you finish. Come play history and renew your affinity for the game. This course simply never gets old.

Double R – Have you ever dreamed of playing Amen Corner? Well, dream no more. If I had to play the same course week after week this might well be the one. Playing this course is like getting that first kiss. You won't ever forget it.

Jodella – Every golfer will thoroughly enjoy their experience here. You'll be hard pressed to pick your favorite hole. The 9th hole, 132 yard, par 3 to an island green, always seems to be a favorite. With overly generous fairways, the big stick should be able to find the short grass. Just watch out for the greens and try to stay below the hole!

Little Leonard – This is a must play golf course. Save your pennies, take on a second job; sell out photos of your girl to your buddies (call me up, I may buy some). Whatever! Just get the money somehow. With length, rolling hills, trees, and trouble everywhere, this course is one that can piss you off and mentally take you out of your game. Just ask The Godfather who found himself 14 putting from #18's, Par 5 fairway. Hey cousin, they have putting greens for that!

The Vokster – Eighteen of the greatest holes in golf. I may not drink while playing this course, just so I can remember them all. There goes my game!

Tour 18

	Par	Yardage	Rating	Slope
Championship	72	7033	74.3	138
Tournament	72	6611	72.2	132
Preferred	72	6202	69.9	127
Forward	72	5493	66.3	119

8718 Amen Corner
Flower Mound, Texas 75022
(817) 430-2000

www.Tour18-Dallas.com

Greens – Bent Grass

Cost of Play – Mon-Thurs $$$ Fri-Sun $$$

Bar/Beverage Cart –

Practice Facility –

Course Grade –

Overall Grade –

Favorite Hole – Hole #9, 132 Yards, Par 3

BEAR CREEK GOLF CLUB

You know that a bear hibernates in the winter. But in this case, the bear never sleeps. Imagine playing a golf course that has a great layout, rolling hills, tons of trees, creeks, water hazards, strategically placed bunkers, short thick rough, fast tight fairways and incredible greens. What could be better than this? How about two of these courses side by side! That's right, at Bear Creek Golf Club there are two great golf courses to choose from: the east course and the west course.

Located in their own forest at DFW Airport, both these layouts require you to think your way around the course. With lots of native trees over rolling terrain and smallish greens, both courses play just under 6700 yards from the tips. A driver is not always necessary, but an accurate tee shot with a long iron or fairway metal is. Many of the holes have trees right on the edges of the fairways, so accuracy is at a premium.

This is the perfect golf course if your old golfing buddy seems to be always out-driving you, but occasionally sprays a shot or two, while you punch it down the middle. Just take him to Bear Creek, it's a safe bet to say that you will probably be stuffing a few of his green backs into your pocket!

The Godfather – Bear Creek is loaded with natural beauty. Rolling hills, great tee boxes, lush green fairways, boulders, ponds, well trimmed bushes, along with great eye candy in the beer carts and at the bar. You will experience nothing but fun at Bear Creek. This is a top-notch facility start to finish, front to back.

Double R – Are you flying in to Dallas to play some good golf? Well, you won't have far to go. If you parachute out of the plane just before it lands, you will land on two of the best courses that the metroplex has to offer. Don't be concerned with picking one course over the other because both are fantastic.

Jodella – The rolling terrain at Bear Creek almost reminds you of being in the hill country of Texas. The facilities are great for eating, drinking and practicing your game. This course has everything to offer, just like a hot date with the old silverback, Jodella!

36

The Vokster – Have you ever ridden on the back of a bear? Well hold on tight or this course will eat you up! If the one you're playing isn't bad enough, they have another course you can try to tame with plenty of trouble to ruin your score. But not to worry, even if you scored badly, you're sure to leave with a smile on your face, provided it doesn't get eaten off.

Bear Creek Golf Club

EAST COURSE

	Par	Yardage	Rating	Slope
Championship	72	6670	72.5	127
Middle	72	6282	71.8	121
Forward	72	5620	72.4	124

WEST COURSE

	Par	Yardage	Rating	Slope
Championship	72	6690	72.7	130
Middle	72	6264	71.8	125
Forward	72	5570	72.5	122

P. O. Box 613108
DFW Airport, Texas 75261-3108
972-456-3200
www.clubcorpgolf.com

Greens – Champion Bermuda

Cost of Play – Mon-Thurs $$ Fri-Sun $$$

Bar/Beverage Cart –

Practice Facility –

East Course Grade –

West Course Grade –

Overall Grade –

Favorite Holes – East Course – Hole #5, 385 Yards, Par 4
West Course – Hole #6, 525 Yards, Par 5

Indian Creek Golf Club

In 1983, the City of Carrollton teamed up with Dick Phelps and Brad Benz to design Indian Creek, their first public golf course. In 1987, Phelps was hired to add a second course. Both 18-hole tracks were premier municipals, cleverly carved out of a forest of hardwoods with an abundance of water to challenge every golfer.

Then in 2003, the City of Carrollton spent over 4 million dollars raising the level of 'The Creeks' course to rival even some of the private courses. They teamed up with Jeff Brauer to completely rework the course, along with major renovations to the pro-shop, clubhouse and the bar. All we can say is, "Wow! What a stroke of genius!"

With changes too numerous to mention, suffice it to say Indian Creek should be at the top of your list. Call early for a tee time at 'The Creeks', but don't be disappointed if you only get to play the 'The Lakes'. Both are well worth your time and money. Either will whet your appetite for a return visit.

The Godfather – If your day is feeling short, come out to Indian Creek. The day can sure get longer here. Hacks need not even attempt this, unless you can get away with hitting from the red tees. In fact, I recommend hacks just stay home, turn on their computer and entertain themselves at www.WhyNotGolf.com. At least you can laugh there.

Double R – With both courses playing over 6,999 yards from the tips, every part of your game will be tested here. 'The Lakes' course has tree lined fairways and plenty of water. 'The Creeks' course is basically the same, but will offer you a little more of a challenge with doglegs and severe bunkering around the greens. No kidding, these oversized, undulating greens will scream for a survey and detailed topographical map. Worse case, don't be afraid to quit early, hit the bar and drown your sorrows.

Little Leonard – This is not a course for the beginner, unless you like chipping out of trees and taking penalties all day. To best envision this course, take Don Kings hairdo and run an electric hair trimmer down the middle of it. That bald path is your fairway.

The Vokster – Can you say T-R-E-E-S? Little Leonard, the sheepherder, has lost many a prize sheep out here. Jodella, the great silverback, feels at home swinging from tree to tree. And Double R's ass got stuck between two trees out here. Luckily, we had 2 carts and a winch that day to free him. Even The Godfather has been known to throw clubs on this track. So if you find lost sheep, lost clubs, boxers with a huge hole in the ass or a big over ripe banana while playing out here, please send them to our office. My playing buddies are always happy to recover their sentimental treasures!

Indian Creek Golf Club

LAKES COURSE

	Par	Yardage	Rating	Slope
Black	72	6999	74.2	129
Blue	72	6532	72.1	125
White	72	5954	69.3	115
Red	72	5271	69.9	119

CREEK COURSE

	Par	Yardage	Rating	Slope
Black	72	7235	74.7	135
Blue	72	6775	72.7	131
White	72	6217	70.1	125
Red	72	5038	64.9	110

1650 West Frankford
Carrollton, Texas 75007
(972) 466-9850

www.indiancreekgolfclub.com

Greens: Lakes Course – Bent Grass   Creek Course – Tiff Eagle

Cost of Play – Mon-Thurs $$ Fri-Sun $$

Bar/Beverage Cart – 🛢 🛢 🛢 🛢 🛢 🛢

Practice Facility – ● ● ● ● ●

Course Grade: Lakes Course – ⚑ ⚑ ⚑   Creek Course – ⚑ ⚑ ⚑ ⚑ ⚑

Overall Grade (Both) – ☆ ☆ ☆ ☆ ☆

Favorite Holes: Lakes Course – Hole #18, 426 Yards, Par 4
                Creek Course – Hole #16, 601 Yards, Par 5

WOODBRIDGE GOLF CLUB

The Goofy Golfers spell Woodbridge, T-R-O-U-B-L-E. But hey, we love trouble, because it offers a great golfing challenge. Birdies and eagles may be great for TV, but at Woodbridge, what we long for are pars and bogeys. This one easily made The Goofy Golfers #6 Best Overall Course and would climb even higher on a list of toughest to play.

Woodbridge has trouble on every hole. The par 3's are not only long in length, but most involve the creek and well-protected greens. Only one par 4 plays under 400 yards on this entire course, so expect to have mid to long irons into every green, even after a well-struck driver. The par 5's are the only holes that you can wedge into for a birdie putt.

So here's the deal, if you want to play adjacent fairways or short unchallenging par 4's, then go to the driving range and play some fantasy golf. If you want to really see what your golf game is all about, then get to Woodbridge. This course gives new meaning to the word demanding.

The Godfather – If your golfing buddy gets overly cocky about his game, take him to Woodbridge for some humbling moments. By the same token, if your own golf game is hurting you may want to re-think playing Woodbridge until your game gets better.

Double R – Woodbridge is long, hard and difficult with plenty of water, trees, and other nasty hazards. If you think you have an "A" game and are ready for the tour, don't brag until you play Woodbridge. Talk about bang for your buck, this course dishes out one hell of a bargain for the challenge it provides.

The Vokster – If you like bamboo shoots driven under your toenails, pain, or torture, go to the BRIDGE! These greens are protected better than a castle with all those moat-like creeks in front of the greens. Leave your Pro-V's in the bag if your game is like The Voksters!

Woodbridge Golf Club

	Par	Yardage	Rating	Slope
Black	72	7056	74.9	137
Blue	72	6411	72.0	131
White	72	5628	67.7	121
Red	72	4981	65.0	108

7400 Country Club Drive
Wylie, Texas 75098
(972) 429-5100
www.WBGolfClub.com

Greens – Tiff Eagle

Cost of Play – Mon-Thurs $$ Fri-Sun $$

Bar/Beverage Cart –

Practice Facility –

Course Grade –

Overall Grade –

Favorite Hole – Hole #13, 614 Yards, Par 5

Lantana Golf Club

If you haven't played this course yet, be warned! Sugar sand infests 87 monster traps at Lantana Golf Club. Deep, soft sand and high faces are the norm. But that's okay! A sandtrap is *supposed* to be a hazard. Playing at 7147 yards from the tips, you better be hitting your mid to long irons well and with so many black hole bunkers to boot, prepare yourself to shoot a higher number than usual.

Half the holes dogleg and several are severe. This adds to the difficulty of the course putting a premium on the placement of your tee ball. The rough is not tall, but it is extremely thick. The tiff eagle greens are some of the best greens you will putt on. One of four feathers in the golf cap of the Flower Mound area, this course is fair but challenging. Unusual because of the inordinate amount of sand, it offers yet another way to truly test your game.

The Godfather – There is almost as much sand as fairway at Lantana. There are a lot of trees and water to contend with, too. A great design left groves and lines of natural trees to buffer the golf course from the houses surrounding the course. The tee boxes are hands down, the best in Dallas. Built perfectly square and maintained as flat as a pool table, if you struggle with getting lined up on a tee box, you won't have to deal with that here.

Double RR – Are 87 total traps enough for your sunbathing pleasure? If you have sunblock, flip-flops and beach towels, you can enjoy half of Cancun only 30 minutes from Dallas. Don't forget your suntan lotion and Speedo when you visit this top-notch course.

Jodella – Do me a favor. When you come out and play, take a pocket full of sand home with you. That way, in about 50 years, there won't be anymore of those damn bunkers left. Some people post a sign warning, 'Beware of Dogs'. At Lantana, they should post a sign that says, 'Beware of Bunkers!'

Little Leonard – The Flower Mound area west of Lewisville has some beautiful terrain filled with rolling hills and plenty of Post Oak trees.

Designed by Jay and Carter Morrish, Lantana is a fun and challenging course for both the high and low handicapper. The most noticeable feature of this course is the traps. If the devil were a sand crab, he would be in heaven here!

The Vokster – Lantana Golf Club is a top-notch facility with a country club atmosphere. The tee boxes have got to be the biggest, squarest, most level ones in the world! The course itself is just immaculate. In fact, the last time I saw something this clean was watching Jodella and Double R polish off their dinner plates!

Lantana Golf Club

	Par	Yardage	Rating	Slope
Black	72	7147	74.2	131
Blue	72	6552	71.1	129
White	72	5933	68.2	121
Red	72	5049	70.1	121

800 Golf Club Drive
Lantana, Texas 76226
(940) 728-GOLF

www.lantanatx.com

Greens – Tiff Eagle

Cost of Play – Mon-Thurs $$ Fri-Sun $$$

Bar/Beverage Cart –

Practice Facility – ⏺ ⏺ ⏺ ⏺ ⏺

Course Grade – ⚑ ⚑ ⚑ ⚑ ⚑

Overall Grade – ☆ ☆ ☆ ☆ ☆

Favorite Hole – Hole #6, 448 Yards, Par 4

43

Twin Lakes Golf Course

Incredibly, Twin Lakes was designed by the landowner. How could someone with no professional help come up with such an impressive design? Adjacent to a tree farm irrigated by the two lakes, this ranks near the top of the most challenging courses we play. It is almost impossible to conquer! One of the large lakes comes into play on 9 of the 18 holes. The other nine holes are cut through the thick east Texas pines.

Looking a little closer, the first three holes are fairly open and easy. But starting with hole number 4, you better be ready to hit some quality golf shots or you will be in for a long day. Trouble lurks on every single shot from this point forward! Most holes will require a mid to long iron into the green, if you have avoided those well placed traps in the fairways. A bad shot into the trees may turn your golf game into a frustrating game of pinball, running up your score with the elusive cup nowhere in sight.

Most golf courses have at least one difficult par 3, but Twin Lakes has two holes (#9, #11) that are so frustrating, they border on the unfair. #9 is 201 yards with water all the way down the right side. Anything left is almost as bad as being in the water itself, because the green slopes so severely toward the lake. On the 214 yard #11, the green is three tiered and about three times as deep as it is wide. The shot is all carry over water. May the force be with you!

The Godfather – Imagine the most horrible, ugly, man-eating monster you can conjure up in your mind! No, I'm not talking about The Vokster. Many things come to mind when talking about this beast. Pain, misery, aggravation. Oh and did I mention pain? Twin Lakes will grip you around the throat on #1 tee and not ease up the pressure until your final putt falls in the hole on #18. One of the best values around in terms of green fees (under $40), you will really appreciate the value when you divide your green fee by your score. If you have a buddy that thinks his game is 'all that' then take him to this obstacle course for a reality check. This is a great, great golf course.

Jodella – This course has everything I don't like; water, trees, sand, length and triple digit scores. The only thing redeeming about it is the choice of two lakes to throw my clubs into when the tally is done.

Little Leonard - Just like Double R without his breath mints, this course is strong and doesn't take long for it to grab your attention. After a few holes you soon realize that hitting a big ball off the tee is only half the battle. With the length you will have left to the flags, and greens protected better than JLo's buttocks, it's like playing a game of darts with a 50 yard throw line.

The Vokster – Gloom, despair and agony on me. Why the hell can't my golf ball see? If there weren't any trouble there would be no fun at all. Oh someone please bring the beer cart to me!

Twin Lakes Golf Course

	Par	Yardage	Rating	Slope
Gold	72	7171	74.4	135
Mens	72	6648	71.4	130
Forward	72	5739	67.2	114
Ladies	72	4964	Na	Na

P. O. Box 816
Canton, Texas 75103
(903) 567-1112

www.TwinLakesGolfCourse.com

Greens – Tiff Eagle

Cost of Play – Mon-Thurs $ Fri-Sun $$

Bar/Beverage Cart –

Practice Facility – ⬤ ⬤ ⬤

Course Grade – ⚑ ⚑ ⚑ ⚑ ⚑

Overall Grade – ☆ ☆ ☆ ☆

Favorite Hole – Hole #11, 214 Yards, Par 3

THE HERITAGE RANCH GOLF AND COUNTRY CLUB

Prepare yourself to be impressed with Heritage Ranch before you even get out of the car. The grounds are beautiful and the staff welcomes you upon arrival. Indicative of what is to come, this impressive country club atmosphere will renew your deep affinity for the game of golf.

Once on the course, expect no less. Serene and comfortable for the most part, this course provides a quiet spacious feel inside the metroplex. It is on these gently rolling hills that The Goofy Golfers have designated hole #16, 'our favorite par 3'. Pristinely scenic, offering no bail out left or right and extremely demanding, this one borders on the unfair. Don't get caught up in the beauty and forget the science of golf. You have to hit a sure and straight ball to prevail here.

Excellent flat tee boxes with short grass are a pleasure to play. Fairways appear to be wide, but once on them, the space is actually outside the fairways. Contrasting rough is deceiving and deeper grass proves to be thick and difficult to exit. Our advice is to avoid it entirely.

The best thing about courses wishing to go private is that they provide for a more relaxed pace. The worst thing is this kind of fun can't last forever. Solidly listed in The Goofy Golfers Best Overall Top 10 Courses to play, be sure to add this one to your list before the opportunity is lost.

The Godfather – I love the elevation changes here, the ups and downs they create constantly change how I address and hit my golf ball. Unfortunately Heritage Ranch is too much golf course for the knuckleheads I play with. Unless the Golf Gods are shining down on Double R…again.

Double R – Play this course with a prevailing south wind. Most of the holes are down wind and a strong north wind would completely change the entire game. So if you don't know the difference between north and south or can't wet your finger and decide which side gets dry first, then go fly a kite.

Jodella – The clubhouse and proshop at Heritage Ranch are awesome.

The clever design affords easy accessibility right down to the putting green and driving range located just outside the clubhouse. I also recommend you make plans to play the course at least twice to truly appreciate what it offers.

The Vokster – I don't usually give this difficult advice to people, but I highly recommend you get to the back tees of the 16th hole relatively sober. Unless of course, your skills improve with suds. It's okay, you can thank me later.

The Heritage Ranch Golf and Country Club

	Par	Yardage	Rating	Slope
Blue	72	6988	73.5	130
White	72	6472	70.9	127
Gold	72	5815	68.0	122
Red	72	4946	69.0	123

465 Scenic Ranch Circle
Fairview, Texas 75069
(972) 549-0276

www.heritageranchgolf.com

Greens – Tiff Eagle

Cost of Play – Mon-Thurs $$ Fri-Sun $$$

Bar/Beverage Cart –

Practice Facility –

Course Grade – ⚑ ⚑ ⚑ ⚑ ⚑

Overall Grade – ☆ ☆ ☆ ☆ ☆

Favorite Hole – Hole #16, 208 Yards, Par 3

GARDEN VALLEY GOLF CLUB

Most golfers have only dreamed about playing Augusta National, where the Masters golf tournament is played every spring. Very few people will ever have that opportunity. Here in Texas, the next best thing is Garden Valley Golf Club.

Located in east Texas, just past Canton this course is set on rolling, sandy terrain along the edges of a pine tree forest. The back nine is especially spectacular to play any time of the year, but the spring or fall seasons are absolutely extraordinary.

Playing only at 6840 yards from the tips, this par 72 course will give up some good scores if you can concentrate on your game and keep it in the fairways. Just a short hop from Dallas, bring the family and rent a cabin on the back 9 to get in a little bass fishing or choose one of their stay and play packages in their "A" frame houses or condos. And if you need more incentives to get out of town, remember that Canton is also famous for their trade days on the weekend before the first Monday of each month. Shopping, fishing, golfing, this spot has it all!

The Godfather – No doubt on how they named this golf course. One of the most beautiful settings in all of Northeast Texas, Garden Valley allows an average golfer the opportunity to score well. However, if you don't keep your ball in the fairway, that garden of beautiful trees can quickly look like a thick maze of briars as you try to hack your way back to the fairway. Don't forget your camera.

Double R – Garden Valley is not long in length, but it does offer a decent challenge. It has several holes with some good elevation changes and the back nine may be the best nine holes around with medium sized, well bunkered greens. You will need an accurate approach shot to score well here.

Jodella – The first 5 holes allow you to get off to a fast start, but from there it definitely gets tougher. Even though only two par 4's play over 400 yards long, it is still a challenging golf course. Just like a beautiful woman, this course can hold you spellbound.

The Vokster – Shots missed into these trees are playable, although hard sand packed ground makes playing out of there a lot tougher. With a fair amount of green side traps and water hazards, Garden Valley is a lot of fun and lower scores can be had, putting a premium on accurate tee shots. After the round enjoy a beverage or two in the cozy bar area. This course was made to truly get away from it all.

Garden Valley Golf Club

	Par	Yardage	Rating	Slope
Back	72	6840	72.4	132
Middle	72	6269	70.1	126
Front	72	5532	72.5	130

22049 FM 1995
Lindale, TX 75771
(903) 882-6107

www.gardenvalleygolfresort.com

Greens – Champion Bermuda

Cost of Play – Mon-Thurs $$ Fri-Sun $$$

Bar/Beverage Cart –

Practice Facility –

Course Grade –

Overall Grade – ☆ ☆ ☆ ☆ ☆

Favorite Hole – Hole #18, 519 Yards, Par 5

CHASE OAKS GOLF CLUB

Located just off Highway 75 in Plano, Chase Oaks offers 27 wonderful holes. The Goofy Golfers have run this track many times and thoroughly enjoy the variation. The Blackjack course has 18 holes. The Sawtooth course has 9, with two sets of tee boxes allowing for 18 full holes of play.

Everyone will experience havoc with the wide creek that twists throughout most of the two courses. Designed by the well-known team of Devlin & Von Hagge, the Blackjack course is shorter on length, but makes up for it in blind shots, variations, open holes, tight holes, doglegs and elevation changes. All four Par 3's play over water, so a par here is a good score. And speaking of water, 15 of the 18 holes have it, so be sure to bring your ball retriever.

Ranked #11 on the 'Best Overall Top 20' list, this course could easily make the top 10 if they would only pay more attention to the conditions. Ownership/management has changed hands numerous times and currently new owners bear the burden of spending more money. It won't keep us from playing it, but we would love to see it get some serious TLC.

Double R – Strategically placed bunkers make the fairways hard to hit. Well-bunkered greens offer a true test for approach shots. This course is visually intimidating off the tees and in the fairways. All in all this is an excellent layout!

Jodella – It doesn't matter how many new courses they build around Dallas, Chase Oaks will still be one of the toughest around. Leave the driver in the bag and hit a long iron or fairway wood for better accuracy. Too bad I can't take my own advice!

The Vokster – Water, water, water. Tee shots over water, approach shots over water, chipping over water, putting over water, well maybe not that, but you get the picture! Why does my ball always seem to covet the attention of the water? I wonder if my swing has anything to do with it? Could it be I just have thirsty balls?

Chase Oaks Golf Club

	Par	Yardage	Rating	Slope
Black	72	6773	74.1	139
Blue	72	6355	71.9	130
White	72	5840	70.5	124
Red	72	5123	70.0	122

7201 Chase Oaks Boulevard
Plano, Texas 75025
(972) 517-7777

www.chaseoaks.com

Greens – Tiff Eagle

Cost of Play – Mon-Thurs $$ Fri-Sun $$

Bar/Beverage Cart –

Practice Facility –

Course Grade –

Overall Grade –

Favorite Hole – Hole #16, 512 Yards, Par 5

THE LINKS AT LANDS END

Located in Yantis, The Links at Lands End is situated on a peninsula in Lake Fork. Home of the Texas record for the biggest large mouth bass caught, it enjoys the distinction of actually being right on the lake. Best of all, you can expect a friendly Texas country welcome from the people who run it.

But what about the course itself? Well, a breeze off Lake Fork makes this a great place to play during the hot Texas summers. A medium length course, natural trees and marsh environment form a layout that will both keep your interest and provide a peaceful experience. Water comes into play on 13 of the last 15 holes, so bring plenty of balls! Doglegs are creative, picturesque and a mental challenge. Natural environment is cleverly used to test even the most practiced game.

Play The Links at Lands End just for the pleasure of it. Well worth even the longest drive from the metroplex, the money you spend on gas will even out with the very reasonable green fees. This course well deserves to be near the top of your must play list and is a real treat to any enthusiast.

The Godfather – Being an avid bass fisherman and golfer, I have died and gone to heaven here. It doesn't get much better than this. As a matter of fact, I am considering retirement, just as soon as this book becomes a bestseller.

Double R – This place is tailor made for Jodella. Just a big ole wide mouthed bass on dry land, our biggest challenge is not to push him in. In fact, he may be the one they talk about that got away!

Jodella – I love courses that are out away from the city. There are no houses, planes overhead, cars honking, trains or sirens; just the occasional sound of a big fish jumping out of the water. And did I mention I tied my best score here with a 78?

The Vokster – Ride shotgun on this course to maximize your viewing pleasure. Fishing and golfing all in one place, you may even consider packing everything up back home, and moving out to Lake Fork. If you do, can I come visit?

The Links At Lands End

	Par	Yardage	Rating	Slope
Gold	71	6664	72.6	130
Blue	71	6100	70.2	129
White	71	5678	70.2	129
Red	71	5068	68.7	114

285 Private Road 5980
Yantis, Texas 75497
(903) 383-3290

www.golflakefork.com

Greens – Tiff Eagle

Cost of Play – Mon-Thurs $$ Fri-Sun $$$

Bar/Beverage Cart –

Practice Facility – 🌐 🌐 🌐

Course Grade – 🏁 🏁 🏁 🏁

Overall Grade – ☆ ☆ ☆ ☆

Favorite Hole – Hole #16, 412 Yards, Par 4

Tierra Verde Golf Club

The City of Arlington received the Audubon International Signature Certification for this golf course. The first municipal course in the world to receive the designation, they can certainly be proud of this prestigious honor. Because of that distinction, playing here is more than just a golf game, it is known all over the world as a place where nature not only thrives, it is appreciated. That alone makes it worth the trip.

The icing on the cake is that Tierra Verde is also an incredible course to play. A top-notch maintenance crew has always kept it in great shape and the facilities are superb. The driving range is lighted and a 3 hole mini practice course may well be their best kept secret. Most holes are pretty secluded, fairways are plenty wide and bordered by the thickest brush around. Golfers who severely slice or hook the ball should definitely bring more or plan to spend some time shopping in the clubhouse.

One of the most well balanced layouts you can play, this course is simply awesome. Two short Par 4's to hit anything from a driver to a 7 iron on, 9 holes that dogleg, nine holes with water and even a Par 3 island green! So don't be shy, 'tee it high and let it fly'. Then after you have found the fairway, just take dead aim at the pin and enjoy the ride.

The Godfather – Wide open fairways are where I shoot my worst scores. How stupid is that? Tierra Verde has a great layout, but I like golf courses that demand a more accurate tee shot. Maybe that's because the strength of my game is my long irons. So for me, this course is about as big a challenge as 'The Vokster' catching a buzz while playing golf.

Double R – Arlington is known for its tourist attractions. Six Flags, Hurricane Harbor, and even the Texas Rangers Ballpark are all located in Arlington. Who would think that just a few miles south of these attractions is 250 acres of secluded, still wild America. Don't be surprised to see a coyote, deer, turkeys or even 'The Great Silverback Jodella' munching on some berries in the briars.

Jodella – If someone blindfolded you, and set you in the middle of the golf course, you would never know that you were in Arlington city limits! It looks more like you were on someone's hunting lease. By the way, if you play here during the spring and summer, don't worry about eating before you come. You'll find plenty of wild fruit growing in the briars, so I never go hungry there.

Tierra Verde Golf Club

	Par	Yardage	Rating	Slope
Black	72	6975	73.3	129
Gold	72	6534	70.9	122
Silver	72	6085	68.6	120
Green	72	5578	72.7	131
Burgundy	72	5111	70.5	119

7005 Golf Club Drive
Arlington, Texas 76001
(817) 478-8500

www.arlingtongolf.com

Greens – Champion Bermuda

Cost of Play – Mon-Thurs $$ Fri-Sun $$$

Bar/Beverage Cart –

Practice Facility –

Course Grade –

Overall Grade –

Favorite Hole – Hole #10, 354 Yards, Par 4

Buffalo Creek Golf Club

Buffalo Creek has always been in immaculate golfing shape and made The Goofy Golfers 'Best Overall Top 20 for the Best Mix of Holes'. Bring all fourteen clubs and every shot in the bag. Boredom will not rear its' ugly head here.

With the exception of only a few holes, the first 14 holes at Buffalo Creek provide a good chance to score. You had better do it then, because the remaining holes here are 'the hardest 4 finishing holes in the metroplex'. Of those, notorious #16 is a 551 yard, Par 5 requiring three pinpoint accurate shots, making it 'the hardest Par 5 in the metroplex'.

Well located for those living in the northeast quadrant of Dallas, it is also worth the trip for those willing to drive a little farther. A good, fair challenge, everyone will find something to brag about here. Noted by The Goofy Golfers for many distinctions, Buffalo Creek should definitely be on your list of places to play.

The Godfather – Expect to get your moneys worth at this well maintained golf course. If you have extra time, Buffalo Creek has one of the better practice facilities in the area, too. The Vokster and Double R really love Buffalo Creek because the beer cart seems to always be on the course.

Jodella – This course is in top condition year round. It gets its name from the creek that runs through the course and comes into play on several of the holes. With wide, generous fairways a herd of buffalo could graze on, good scores can be had.

The Vokster – Yeah, they got the hardest four finishing holes, but what's really important is that they have the 16 ouncers to help ease the pain. But don't count the ounces because I, The Great Vokster, have declared this course the '6-16'er'. Now that's an 'ice downer' I can get into.

Buffalo Creek Golf Club

	Par	Yardage	Rating	Slope
Championship	71	7018	73.8	133
Back	71	6476	70.7	125
Middle	71	5863	67.5	114
Forward	71	5209	67.0	113

624 Country Club Drive
Heath, Texas 75032
(972) 771-4003

www.americangolf.com

Greens – Champion Bermuda

Cost of Play – Mon-Thurs $$ Fri-Sun $$$

Bar/Beverage Cart –

Practice Facility –

Course Grade –

Overall Grade – ☆ ☆ ☆ ☆

Favorite Hole – #16, 551 Yards, Par 5

Tenison Park Golf Course

Historically, Tenison Park goes back to 1925 and is the home of legends like Lee Trevino, Titanic Thompson and Lee Elder. A second course (now named 'The Glen') was added to the park in the 1950's. Originally hallowed ground to some, Tenison Park suffered neglect over the years, but rallied back through a significant renovation to the west course in 2000. Currently known as 'Tenison Highlands', the west course is clearly one of the top municipal courses in Dallas and has set the standard for other city owned courses.

D. A. Weibring is responsible for the layout design changes and improved reputation of this facility, proving Dallas has finally come to understand the value of a well-built course. Severe elevation changes, the new large undulating greens, big thick trees and many more bunkers make this a must play municipal for every golfer. If you haven't played it since the changes, you will be amazed at the difference! But don't take our word for it, play it and see for yourself.

The Godfather – What a really awesome municipal for Dallas. The practice area has covered tee boxes available to improve your swing come rain or shine. Located right by a teaching facility, it is an easy walk to test out a new club or buy another bucket of balls. Boosted by this improved course, the surrounding area is starting to improve and it can't happen soon enough to enhance this facility. Dallas should be commended for putting money into a depressed area and salvaging such a historic place.

Double R – This is where I learned to play golf. When I was growing up, it was 'the place' to play. Guess I'm a little sentimental about it, but hey, so is Lee Trevino!

Jodella – What great memories this course brings back. I can remember standing in line at 5:00 on Thursday morning to get a weekend tee time. Those days are long gone, but the memories will always remain. Never say 'the Great Silverback' is not a softie about golf .

The Vokster – This course can finally pat itself on the back just like The Godfather does all the time. The only difference is they have the right too! A new facelift did this course wonders. I think I'll take it upon myself to fix The Godfather's.

Tenison Park Golf Course

TENISON GLEN

	Par	Yardage	Rating	Slope
Gold	72	6605	71.2	122
Blue	72	6287	69.6	117
White	72	5877	67.7	113
Red	72	5107	70.8	115

TENISON HIGHLANDS

	Par	Yardage	Rating	Slope
Diamond	72	7078	73.9	129
Gold	72	6610	71.6	124
Silver	72	5905	68.2	119
Pearl	72	4883	68.3	114

3501 Samuel Boulevard
Dallas, Texas 75223
(214) 670-1402

www.TenisonPark.com

Greens:
Tenison Glen – Bermuda   Tenison Highlands – Tiff Eagle
Cost of Play: Tenison Glen – Mon-Thurs $ Fri-Sun $$
          Tenison Highlands – Mon-Thurs $$ Fri-Sun $$
Bar/Beverage Cart –
Practice Facility –
Course Grade: Tenison Glen –   Tenison Highlands
Overall Grades -

Favorite Holes: Tenison Glen - Hole #2, 501 Yards, Par 5
          Tenison Highlands – Hole #3, 625 Yards, Par 5

PINE DUNES RESORT AND GOLF CLUB

Set in a forest of tall pines and other native trees, the terrain on this course will have you believing you are in South Carolina. Natural sandy soil lends itself to prevalent native grasses and sand dunes. Architect Jay Morrish, did an impressive job with the design, blending in a great mixture of both length and shape. Sand dunes set this course apart from all the others. So whether in the dunes or the fairways, don't expect to get a flat lie.

One of the hidden hazards at Pine Dunes is the area between the fairways and the edge of the trees. It is very difficult for grass to grow in the shaded areas leaving you to contend with hard-packed sandy lies. If you are lucky enough to have a shot around or through the trees, your approach shot will be difficult to keep on the green.

With minimal water hazards and out-of-bounds, you might think this is an easy course to score on. However, the powerful pines, sandy dunes and yardage over 7100, still provides plenty of trouble out there to test your game. This course is ranked #16 on The Goofy Golfers Best Overall Top 20 list and should be on your short list of places to play.

The Godfather – Although the pro shop and practice areas are nothing to write home about, the golf course surely is. I love bringing my short hitting buddies here because I prevail in l-e-n-g-t-h and accuracy.

Double R – Pine Dunes has some of the finest tee boxes you will ever play on. They are level and visually appealing. You need to enjoy these level lies, because you won't see any more out on the course.

Jodella – You'll love the privacy of this course. With no houses around, you can throw clubs and cuss all you want, and no one will see you or hear you! Not that I would stoop to that kind of behavior myself.

The Vokster – Sand, sand, sand. This whole course is a hazard! The last time I saw this much sand I was wearing a twelve pack and a Speedo. Sadly, I didn't score well there either!

Pine Dunes Resort and Golf Club

	Par	Yardage	Rating	Slope
Gold	72	7117	74.4	131
Blue	72	6537	71.3	126
White	72	5819	68.1	119
Red	72	5150	72.0	127

159 Private Road 7019
Frankston, Texas 75763
(903) 876-4336

www.pinedunes.com

Greens – Tiff Eagle

Cost of Play – Mon-Thurs $$ Fri-Sun $$$

Bar/Beverage Cart –

Practice Facility – ⬤

Course Grade – ⚑ ⚑ ⚑ ⚑

Overall Grade – ☆ ☆ ☆

Favorite Hole – Hole #4, 463 Yards, Par 4

THE GOLF CLUB AT McKINNEY

Entrepreneur Jerry Jones and former NFL player, Jim Lindsey, teamed up to open The Golf Club at McKinney and surrounding residential compound. Currently semi-private, they prefer to cater to members, but the public can generally secure a tee time during the week. However, with fast growth well underway, those wishing to play this course will have to beat the ultimate rush to go private.

Destined to be legendary, in our opinion the very first hole holds the distinction of 'the most difficult landing area in the metroplex'. Featuring an extremely demanding tee shot, this one is frequently visited by choice words and the overused mulligan. Don't be discouraged. By far the course loosens up after that brutal ice breaker.

Plenty of variation is prevalent throughout the course. Distinctive moguling between holes is out of the ordinary and serves to separate parallel holes. Arguably some of the toughest greens, three putts are a norm and 4 are entirely possible. But that's the worst of it, because the rest of the course is extremely doable and will culminate in a surprisingly easy finish.

The Godfather – Go to the driving range first and then warm up on the putting green. Also, remember to wear your Goofy Golfer padded hat on this course. The flying putter is a frequent visitor here. It's so bad for Jodella, he has to bring along an extra one just in case he makes a wet hole in one.

Double R – Huge mounds, broken tree lines, hundreds of newly planted trees and elevated greens. Talk about looks being deceiving – the scorecard hole layout on this course looks like a walk in the park – but in reality, they left out the muggers, drunks and thieves. Hello 'Golf Club At McKinney'! Have a little mercy. Provide some more details so I don't go to this gunfight with a knife.

Jodella – A fairly demanding golf course, it is probably more suited for the low to mid handicapped golfer. So it looks like 'the old silverback' won't be coming back to this track on a regular basis, as I am highly handicapped. Not to mention that I have to play with these other three dummies.

The Vokster – Apparently they built this course with me in mind. Surrounded by apartments, I can drink, play, drink, drink and order one more for the short walk home. Best of all, I can save the money I would have spent on a designated driver to drink and play another day. Note to Apartment Management: When the first floor unit closest to the 19th hole becomes available, please call me first.

The Golf Club At McKinney

	Par	Yardage	Rating	Slope
Blue	72	6857	73.0	138
White	72	6188	70.0	128
Gold	72	5468	66.2	123
Red	72	4849	67.2	117

3191 Medical Center Drive, Building G
McKinney, Texas 75069

(972) 540-6880

www.lindseymanagement.com

Greens – Tiff Eagle

Cost of Play – Mon-Thurs $$ Fri-Sun $$$

Bar/Beverage Cart –

Practice Facility –

Course Grade –

Overall Grade

Favorite Hole – Hole #1, 550 Yards, Par 5

WESTRIDGE GOLF COURSE

Westridge is different than any other golf course in the metroplex because it has three par 3's, three par 4's and three par 5's on each nine. Playing at 7043 yards, this par 72 layout has over 40 bunkers and water on 8 of the 18 holes. In other words, this is fun to play!

The fairways are very generous with plenty of width. However, all of the par 4's and 5's have either a fairway bunker or some type of water. In keeping with the usual Jeff Brauer calling cards, these greens are large undulating and sloping. Therefore, we highly recommend keeping your ball below the hole on the greens or three putts will be the norm. With 6 par 3's and 6 par 5's, low scores should be routine, but never mundane.

Expect this course to blossom with more improvements to the bar and grill area. In the next few years, houses filling in around it will also significantly change the overall look. Conveniently located just west of McKinney, Westridge promises to become one of your favorite courses to play.

The Godfather – Housing developments are filling up all around Westridge and it is no wonder why. A great golf course and improving amenities clearly make it one of the metroplex favorites to play. For tee times call early! Beat the suburban rush.

Double R – What I really like about this course is the number 6. 6 par 3's, 6 par 4's, 6 par 5's and 6 Bud Lights. It doesn't get any better than that!

Jodella – Anal golfers like me will appreciate how the scorecard tears off and becomes your personal yardage chart. Indicative of the extra details in this course, it is like having your own personal caddie in your back pocket. And with the way I hit my driver, I need it to help me find my way back to the fairways.

The Vokster – If they really want to help me out, how about 9 par 3's and 9 par 5's. The fewer the par 4's the better. But then par 4's are what drove me to drinking, so maybe not.

Westridge Golf Course

	Par	Yardage	Rating	Slope
Black	72	7043	74.0	131
Blue	72	6651	72.0	127
White	72	6004	68.6	115
Red	72	5242	70.8	120

9055 Cotton Ridge Road North
McKinney, Texas 75070
(972) 346-2212

www.westridgegolfcourse.com

Greens – Tiff Eagle

Cost of Play – Mon-Thurs $$ Fri-Sun $$

Bar/Beverage Cart –

Practice Facility –

Course Grade –

Overall Grade –

Favorite Hole – Hole #9, 456 Yards, Par 4

BRIDLEWOOD GOLF CLUB

Voted 'the number one bent grass greens in the Dallas area' the past three years, Bridlewood has a country club appeal with public course fees. Set on gently rolling terrain, this D. A. Weibring design winds through an award winning subdivision past pristine wrought iron fencing that actually adds to the overall beauty. For the past several years, this course has hosted the 'WBAP Golf Course Challenge' to break the world record for the fastest round of golf. It hasn't happened yet, but it certainly could with the flat, fast greens.

Good scores can be had on this course for any handicap player. Only a handful of holes demand a well-placed tee shot. The remaining holes offer wide, generous fairways allowing plenty of room for error. Although OB comes into play, it is set so far off the fairways most bad tee shots will not reach it. Water is evident all over the back nine, but comes into play on just a few holes.

Bridlewood may well have the largest driving range in the Dallas public golf community and boasts a very impressive practice area and facility. Looking for a place to call home? Convenient to shopping, DFW airport, entertainment, some of the best schools in Texas and in the heart of metroplex golfing, here is where your search could end.

Double R – If you like to play golf courses that are open and have lots of room, Bridlewood is your choice. Don't let the openness fool you though, at 7,111 yards there is still enough length to test your game.

Jodella – The greens are a tad on the bigger side, just like The Vokster's stomach, but they're fairly flat. With not a lot of mounding and bent grass, putting should be a pleasure.

Little Leonard – Another great D.A. Weibring design! The course plays well for golfers with a handicap from 0-30, (basically from the range of me to The Vokster). The course is forgiving for the beginner, but can jump up and bite the low handicapper right square in the knickers. Take the time to appreciate the trees throughout this course. And leave yourself time to enjoy the clubhouse, restaurant and bar.

The Vokster – The front 9 finishes with 2 demanding holes, a par 3 playing to195 yards with all carry over water. The Par 4, 9th hole is one of the hardest handicapped holes on the course. Playing just over 7100 yards in length, you will definitely need to "Drive For Show" and "Putt For Dough" here.

Bridlewood Golf Club

	Par	Yardage	Rating	Slope
Black	72	7111	73.6	130
Blue	72	6557	71.0	123
White	72	6061	68.5	117
Red	72	5278	70.7	120

4000 Windsor Drive
Flower Mound, Texas 75028
972-355-4800

www.bridlewoodgolf.com

Greens – Bent Grass

Cost of Play – Mon-Thurs $$ Fri-Sun $$$

Bar/Beverage Cart –

Practice Facility –

Course Grade –

Overall Grade –

Favorite Hole – Hole #13, 568 Yards, Par 5

THE GOLF CLUB AT CASTLE HILLS

Opened in the late 1990's, this Morrish Brothers design is one of the finer clubs in the metroplex. Located on the southeast edge of Lewisville, it is easily accessible from I-35 and convenient to most of the north Dallas area. Built in conjunction with an upscale subdivision, it boasts a unique clubhouse as well as a challenging course and could easily be included in your list of favorites.

After the first two holes on the front nine, escape from the trees and play your game alongside a lot of water and natural wetlands. While the front nine is fairly open with generous fairways, large elevated greens and numerous well-placed bunkers, it is the back nine that will truly test your skill. Opening with a 479 yard, Par 4, a 601 yard Par 5 and a 242 yard, Par 3, the back nine winds through the trees, plays tighter and will not let up right through the risk/reward 18th hole.

Even from the middle or up tees, Castle Hills will demand your 'A' game. In fact, just as soon as they tighten up the fairways and let the rough grow higher, this course could easily host a PGA Tour event. So here's the warning: Bring the ringer, but have mercy and leave the hack at home!

The Godfather – Amateurs should play the preferred tees. Laced with penalty areas, this is a super layout with a good mix of Par 3's. If the trees and traps aren't enough, there is thick and I mean thick, clumpy grass just outside the fairways. But on the other hand, there are a whole lot of places to 'relieve' yourself.

Double R – If you live in the Lewisville area and don't play golf, will you please move so someone who does play can move into your house? How lucky they would be! No less than 7 of The Goofy Golfer Top 20 courses are within shouting distance of each other. Castle Hills is just the tip of the iceberg, so call your Realtor and pack your golf bag, this is the place to be.

The Vokster – Castle Hills golf course is top notch, complete with practice area, driving range and a clubhouse boasting lush panoramic views. The golf course itself is beautifully laid out through native terrain, environmental areas, and subtle rolling and turning land. Ice down a couple of extra cold ones, you'll be swilling with the best of them on this bad boy.

The Golf Club At Castle Hills

	Par	Yardage	Rating	Slope
Gray	72	7152	74.3	139
Gold	72	6607	71.8	127
Blue	72	6191	69.7	117
Red	72	5481	71.4	119
Green	72	5064	N/A	N/A

699 Lady Of The Lake Boulevard
Lewisville, Texas 75056
(972) 899-7400

www.castlehillsgolfclub.com

Greens – Bent Grass

Cost of Play – Mon-Thurs $$$ Fri-Sun $$$

Bar/Beverage Cart –

Practice Facility –

Course Grade –

Overall Grade –

Favorite Hole – Hole #10, 479 Yards, Par 4

REVIEWS
THE REST OF THE FIELD

AAKI Ranch International Golf Course

Ever have a fantasy about creating your own golf course? Welcome to AAKI Ranch. Out there, life is laid back and the object is simple: These boys just want to play some golf and they had a little extra pasture left over. Exit the cows and enter the cup flags. This one is a keeper.

Seriously, in every sport there are extremes and AAKI easily fits in that category. Greens are relatively small and can you say flat? One can only hope that one day this little course that can will grow up and actually be one that could.

In the meantime, put on your chaps and come on out. This international place has to be seen to be believed.

The Godfather – Howdy! How you doin'? Are you feeling the flavor of AAKI? The stereotypical course for cow pasture pool, scattered with old watering holes and missing only the four-legged t-bones. Back and forth, eight holes actually run side by side with scattered saplings to form the edges of these spacious fairways. The only thing missing here are tighter fairways, taller rough, 50 or so bunkers, deeper ponds, water in the creeks and undulating greens. But there is hope! Because by golly they've gone and bought some ball washers.

Double R – Definitely for the low budget golfer. If you can't afford golf shoes, just step out of that pickup truck in your roughed up cowboy boots and get on with the playing. And should you find yourself with no balls, don't worry! You can probably go out into the dried up ditch bed and just dig up a few.

The Vokster – If you have never turned over a couple of cool ones while playing pasture pool, I highly advise you to try it here. Ain't nothing better than downing a couple of beers while the local moo cows look at you with a bewildered face. Or maybe they are just waiting to see if you will pop that ball in your mouth to clean it. Hey, somebody's got to have a little fun out here.

AAKI Ranch International Golf Course

	Par	Yardage	Rating	Slope
Back	71	6524	69.4	114
Middle	71	6044	68.0	110
Front	71	5101	68.4	113

846 FM 2453
Royce City, Texas 75189
972-636-2254

www.AAKIRanch.com

Greens - Bermuda

Cost of Play – Mon-Thurs $ Fri-Sun $$

Bar/Beverage Cart –

Practice Facility –

Course Grade –

Overall Grade –

Favorite Hole – #18, Par 5, 480 Yards

CEDAR CREST GOLF COURSE

Cedar Crest has been around for a long time. In fact, they hosted a PGA Championship in 1927. Time honored and filled with local golfing history, Lee Trevino used to play among the trees that are now massive oaks.

Last year, Cedar Crest closed to make way for an overall renovation by the very respected D. A. Weibring. Reopened in October of 2004, the City of Dallas is expected to spend in excess of 5 million dollars adding in a driving range, new clubhouse, complete short game practice facility, in excess of 20 bunkers and overall reshaping of the course.

There is no such thing as a flat spot at Cedar Crest! Built on the side of a hill, rolling terrain provides an open feel, but the course doesn't play that way. Even the most seasoned golfer will find a challenge here and we eagerly anticipate playing this new design. The City of Dallas should be applauded for making this great course even better!

The Godfather - Expect this course to stay pristine all year round with the addition of a sprinkler system. And one of the signatures of D. A. Weibring is that he gets the cart paths out of the fairways and into the trees. Now The Vokster and Double R can find their balls a little quicker.

Double R – Playing this course brings back a lot of old memories for me. A coworker taught me to play this wonderful game here and I've been hooked on it every since. My physique may have changed a little bit, but my love for the game has not.

Jodella – A famous tree on #7 was nicknamed Willie Mays because of all the tee shots it caught. It was taken out, but they added two bunkers to replace it. And talk about a view! Standing on the #15 tee box, you can see reunion tower over the green. Awesome!

The Vokster – This course should drive you nuts with all the uneven lies. How can a course that looks so open play so tight? And thank goodness for carts! I need to work on my six pack abs, but no way would I want to walk this bad boy.

Cedar Crest Golf Course

	Par	Yardage	Rating	Slope
Black	71	6505	71.7	133
Gold	71	6104	69.3	128
Silver	71	5628	67.6	123
Burgundy	71	4969	N/A	N/A

1800 Southerland Avenue
Dallas, Texas   75203
(214) 670-7615

www.golfindallas.net

Greens – Tiff Dwarf Bermuda

Cost of Play – Mon-Thurs $$ Fri-Sun $$

Bar/Beverage Cart –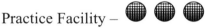

Practice Facility –

Course Grade – ⚑ ⚑ ⚑ ⚑

Overall Grade – ☆ ☆ ☆ ☆

Favorite Hole – Hole #3, 202 Yards, Par 3

Chester W. Ditto Golf Course

Don't judge a book by its cover or a golf course by its name! A name like Chester Ditto might conjure up images of 'Billy-Bob-Hick' in his overalls, straw hat and donkey building a golf course with a worn out plow. But this is definitely not a goat ranch! Short and commanding, it is player friendly and high handicappers will love it.

The City of Arlington has included a decent practice area in this municipal course, especially appealing to golfers still working on their game. A good value for your golfing dollar, you can't ask for a better way to wile away a day. So get over the name, grab your bag and go out to the 'Ditto' for a round or two. And hey, if wearing a straw hat helps your game, bring it on. Just leave the donkey at home, 'cause they 'got carts'.

The Godfather – Expect to see light-rolling terrain, tight fairways and some well-protected greens. Avoid long shots or going over on the greens, because many of them are sloping on the backside to groves of briars and trees like those Jodella, the great silverback was conceived in. So bring extra balls, because retrieval is out of the question. After all, there are likely to be more great-silverback-gorilla's lurking in there.

Double R – Several of the holes have some rolling terrain that makes the hole play a little more difficult. Most of the greens are very small, so every approach shot that stays on the green will leave you a good birdie putt. Seize the Ditto; don't let this opportunity pass you by.

Jodella – What a surprise! Chester Ditto is a pretty good golf course that doesn't really get started until the 5th hole. You had better get off to a good start, because the back 9 is set in a grove of small native oak trees, over rolling, sloping terrain and even a well struck shot might bounce and roll its' way into trouble. Nothing makes 'the old silverback' mad quicker than a well-hit shot that goes looking for trouble.

The Vokster – Obviously, I don't bother reviewing courses that don't sell beer.

C. W. Ditto Golf Course

	Par	Yardage	Rating	Slope
Blue	72	6726	70.8	117
White	72	6117	68.5	112
Red	72	5546	71.3	118

801 Brown Boulevard
Arlington, Texas 76011
(817) 275-5941

www.arlingtongolf.com

Greens – Bermuda

Cost of Play – Mon-Thurs $ Fri-Sun $$

Bar/Beverage Cart – No Cans!

Practice Facility –

Course Grade –

Overall Grade –

Favorite Hole – Hole #15, 494 Yards, Par 5

Country View Golf Club

The City of Lancaster has a course they can be proud of in Country View. A Ron Garl design, at first glance, this 6419 yard par 71 golf course looks like a piece of cake. But a closer look reveals a unique golf course with water on 13 out of 18 holes. Every green is well elevated and you will have your hands full keeping your score in check.

The key to trouble here is easily the creek and lakes. Winding around and coming into play on almost every hole, if the water doesn't get you, the mature trees in and around it will. A shot makers paradise, this track is well thought out and lacks only length to make it a major contender.

Bring your long knocking buddies out here and watch them squirm their way through these tight fairways. What a hoot! Length is not a premium here, but accuracy surely is. Packed with tons of eye appeal, this municipal course provides a lot of bang for the buck.

The Godfather – Boy, if this course had 400 or 500 more yards it would be one bad motor scooter. Tee boxes and greens are elevated because of the major creek that was used so well on this course. Water is all over the place to gobble up errant balls. I am even going to be so bold as to say that the approach shots here are the most difficult in the area. Balls that are hit just right or left of the green will ricochet off the sides of those elevated greens to water hazards below.

Double R – If you don't have a brain or don't like using the one you have then don't play here. This course will require you to think about every single shot. Your undivided attention will be needed throughout the round to score well here.

Jodella – Why are they filling in the bunkers with grass? So they don't have to maintain them. What a shame! This course has the potential to be great, but no! It is all about the money. Add two dollars back to the green fee and put the bunkers back in! Avoid the slide into mediocrity, Lancaster and get a clue before it is too late.

The Vokster – I usually don't like courses that appear a little too open, however, just walking to and from these greens makes me feel like I have a good buzz on. Who needs beer?

Country View Golf Club

	Par	Yardage	Rating	Slope
Gold	71	6419	71.0	128
Blue	71	5813	69.8	122
White	71	5231	68.6	116
Red	71	4653	67.8	110

240 West Beltline
Lancaster, Texas   75146
(972) 227-0995

www.CountryviewGolfCourse.com

Greens – Bermuda

Cost of Play – Mon-Thurs $ Fri-Sun $$

Bar/Beverage Cart –

Practice Facility – ⬤ ⬤ ⬤

Course Grade – 🏳 🏳 🏳

Overall Grade – ☆ ☆

Favorite Hole – Hole #17, 519 Yards, Par 5

Coyote Ridge Golf Club

'Wild enough to intrigue you, tame enough to bring you back!' That's the slogan at Coyote Ridge. Very few courses can claim two distinctively different nines, but Coyote Ridge has that and more. Practically barren of trees on the front nine, it has many characteristics of a links-style golf course. Conversely, a natural creek becomes prevalent on the back nine and will have you begging for some elbow room.

If you can manage to stay out of the fairway traps, the front nine should be easier to score on than the back. Dominated by water on six holes, clearly only the dry ball will prevail. Use that warm-up to your advantage, because the back nine brings a whole different visual perspective to the game. Woven through an old rock quarry, the 10th hole will immediately set the tempo for the back nine. Shorter but straighter off the tee players should use the changes to your advantage, but don't be lulled, nothing on this course is set in stone.

The Godfather – There is 640 yards difference between the back tee box and the next tee box up. The front nine is a little more open than the back, but it still plays tough with only a few scattered well-positioned big trees and enough sand to build another middle-eastern country. Get ready big boy, there's more trouble on the back and that's when the coyotes really start to howl.

Double R – With a great facility, practice round and pavilion, Coyote Ridge is definitely a must to play. This is one of Jodella's favorite courses because it is built the same way he likes his women, big with lots of mounds.

Jodella – Playing at only 6795 yards long from the tips, it seems short by today's standards but take a look again; it's only a par 71! Add in a couple 100 yards to compensate for only one par 5 on the front and you have a really good test of skill. With about 40 bunkers to choose from you're sure to find your favorite. Notice between holes #2 and #8, there are 6 smaller bunkers. There used to be only 5, but after a few of the Vokster's famous fat KA-THWOP shots, they decided to fill in the divot with sand and now you have 6.

Little Leonard – This is one fun track. Every hole has character and will hold your attention throughout. Designer George Williams takes full advantage of the natural terrain with a decent amount of elevation change throughout the course. I like the way the water is left in its natural state with reeds and cattails throughout. Texas winds prevail here, so plan for the worst. Sorry Jodella, this course makes you think.

Coyote Ridge Golf Club

	Par	Yardage	Rating	Slope
Black	71	6795	72.8	130
Blue	71	6155	69.3	123
White	71	5705	66.8	115
Red	71	4995	70.0	122

1680 Bandera Drive
Carrollton, Texas 75010
(972) 939-0666

www.coyoteridgegolf.com

Greens – Champion Bermuda

Cost of Play – Mon-Thurs $$ Fri-Sun $$

Bar/Beverage Cart –

Practice Facility –

Course Grade –

Overall Grade – ☆☆☆☆

Favorite Hole – Hole #10, 590 Yards, Par 5

CREEKVIEW GOLF CLUB

There is actually an exit right off Highway 175 in Crandall especially for this golf course. But beware, it is not a true exit ramp and if you are not careful you'll be the chip shot on the first hole. If you miss it, there is a long drive to the next exit. Don't give in to the frustration; just consider it a warm up for the long drives that are mandatory at Creekview.

This one has potential, but falls considerably short of realizing it. Caught in a catch-22 lease/ownership deal with the City of Crandall, no real relief is in site and those seeking a new place to play should realize it sorely lacks in character. But hey, Creekview plays out at over 7200 yards from the blue tees and the up tees play over 1000 shorter, providing a reasonably priced way to hone your game. Only three holes have any significant elevation to them and all are par 4's playing either up or down the one small hill. A few scattered ponds and one small creek come into play, so if you loose many balls here, you may need to consider a new sport.

With minimal elevation change and very few hazards, low scores are the norm. In fact, the resident pro, Tim Lawson, actually made the Guinness Book of World Records by shooting a 58 on this par 72 golf course. He really had 12 birdies and one eagle! Improve your own golfing resume. Breaking 60 here is obviously possible if you've got game.

Double R – Open fairways, few trees, only a few water hazards and easy to putt greens will allow for good scoring here. In fact, if you can't score here, I suggest you visit your local bar. The greens are as flat as a pancake. One tip: Bring syrup.

Jodella – A really long course that just does not play to the length it shows on the scorecard. It doesn't matter where you hit the ball; you still have a shot back to the green. It's a shame the traps and bunkers are not maintained. Crandall, I smell opportunity! Can you? Well-placed money here would make all the difference.

The Vokster – You want to go low on a long course? Smash away from the tees and fear not! You will almost always have a shot in. If you get a little bored, load up a few extra cans of liquid gold for a more entertaining back nine. Hey wait; this is my kind of place! Because sober or sloshed, you are always a winner here.

Creekview Golf Club

	Par	Yardage	Rating	Slope
Blue	72	7238	74.1	119
White	72	6161	68.7	110
Red	72	5459	71.2	115

1602 East Highway 175
Crandall, Texas 75114
(972) 472-8400

www.creekviewgolfclub.net

Greens – Bent Grass

Cost of Play – Mon-Thurs $ Fri-Sun $$

Bar/Beverage Cart –

Practice Facility –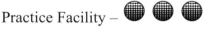

Course Grade –

Overall Grade –

Favorite Hole – Hole #18, 468 Yards, Par 4

EAGLE ROCK GOLF CLUB
(Formerly The Summit)

You won't believe this story! Rocky Carlson and a buddy were going to play golf at a local course, but it was so crowded, they decided to head down the road to play 'The Summit' in Ennis. After nine holes, Rocky lost seven balls that were hit in the middle of the fairway, because the grass was so thick and not maintained. He quit after nine holes and complained loudly to the management asking for his money back. When he got home, he pulled up the course tax records on the Internet and located the owner. He then wrote an email to the owner, making him an offer to buy the course. Two weeks later, he became the new owner.

We were unable to review this as an active course, because it is under serious renovation. But Rocky Carlson plans to reopen as Eagle Rock in April of 2005. Drastic changes are already underway. Tee boxes are being moved, a rocky stream is being added, the clubhouse will be remodeled and the course itself is being redesigned.

Enthusiastic and willing to put in a lot of hard work, Carlson's course has a lot of potential. Clearly, if the renovations he has planned come to fruition, Eagle Rock will be a reasonable and enjoyable course for the Ennis area. Always happy to see another course get a facelift, we wish Rocky well and look forward to teeing off on the new track.

The Godfather – Traveling south on 45 from Dallas, look to the east when reaching Garrett. Don't let the three holes you can see fool you, the rest have much potential for a challenging game.

Jodella – The front nine is the best as it wraps around Parker Hill, the highest point from Ennis to Austin in the hill country – 531 feet above sea level. Aptly named after Bonnie and Clyde, who used the hill as a hideout because of the panoramic view, it lends an air of historical fun to the game. Thank you Rocky Carlson for not letting another course go to waste.

The Vokster – Looking forward to playing another golf course that is in the process of bringing major changes to its facility. Yes! The beloved liquor license!

Eagle Rock Golf Club (Formerly The Summit)

Par and Yardage are approximate because of renovations. Rating and Slope are currently not available.

	Par	Yardage	Rating	Slope
Blue	72	6702	NA	NA
White	72	6125	NA	NA
Gold	72	5264	NA	NA
Red	72	4538	NA	NA

102 Crescentview Drive
Ennis, Texas 75119
(972) 878-4653

www.eaglerockgolfclub.com

Greens – Champion Dwarf

Cost of Play – Mon-Thurs $ Fri-Sun $

Bar/Beverage Cart –

Practice Facility –

Course Grade –

Overall Grade –

Favorite Hole – Waiting On Course Completion

FIREWHEEL GOLF PARK

Firewheel Golf Park opened up in 1983 and for a long time was one of the must play courses in the Dallas area. But in the mid 80's, golf started to really boom and the City of Garland opened up another course on the property. The new course was then aptly referred to as 'The Lakes', indicative of the generous water hazards scattered throughout. The original course became known as 'The Old Course'.

In 2002, the City of Garland opened up 27 more holes at this site, called 'The Bridges'. This new course has a separate proshop, bar/grill and driving range. The original two courses share a set of those amenities, making this facility the only one in the metroplex with this many luxuries to enjoy. During the same improvement phase, 'The Lakes' was re-arranged and is now entirely different. Most of the new holes lie in a low area and all of the greens are elevated, some severely. Hitting your approach shots to these greens is a premium.

Currently with 63 holes to offer the avid golfer, Firewheel is the largest golfing facility in the Dallas area. That means more available tee times and less congestion. Well rounded from beginner to professional, Firewheel definitely has what it takes to appeal to any golfer.

The Godfather – Garland may not know how to structure a road system in and out of their beloved town, but they do know how to spend money on a golf course. Most holes are golfer friendly with wide fairways, big drop zones and average to large greens. My favorite 18 at Firewheel is still the original 18 holes. I like that layout best because it has a good mix of everything and offers professional yardage at Par 71. An abundance of white shale rock lies very close to the surface in this area of North Garland. Creeks that work their way throughout the golf course are carved through these shale rock layers and are actually clean. I didn't miss the usual Texas mud holes at all!

Jodella – A place fair enough to take your family for a great time, but also challenging enough to give even the low handicapper a run for his money. Firewheel is an impressive example and has definitely set the standard for municipal courses in the metroplex.

The Vokster – Firewheel offers 63 holes of golf to fill even the biggest of appetites. But looking at the spread on Jodella and Double R, Firewheel may want to add extra holes. Those two blubber boys never get their fill!

Firewheel Golf Park

OLD COURSE

	Par	Yardage	Rating	Slope
Gold	71	7054	74.1	135
Blue	71	6429	71.6	131
White	71	6054	69.9	124
Red	71	5497	N/A	N/A

LAKES COURSE

	Par	Yardage	Rating	Slope
Gold	72	7134	75.5	139
Blue	72	6680	73.6	134
White	72	6141	70.7	125
Red	72	5502	73.6	126

(CONTINUED ON NEXT PAGE)

Firewheel Golf Park (Continued)

The Bridges course consists of 3 different nines: The Champion, The Tradition and The Masters. Together they can be mixed to create three completely different courses.

THE CHAMPION

	Par	Yardage	Rating	Slope
Gold	36	3474	36.8	130
Blue	36	3236	35.4	127
White	36	2902	33.9	123
Red	36	2614	35.9	122

THE TRADITION

	Par	Yardage	Rating	Slope
Gold	35	3202	35.5	130
Blue	35	2985	34.6	127
White	35	2801	33.9	122
Red	35	2529	35.8	129

THE MASTERS

	Par	Yardage	Rating	Slope
Gold	36	3553	37.5	138
Blue	36	3320	36.5	134
White	36	2946	34.6	129
Red	36	2529	36.4	122

Old and Lake Course

600 West Campbell
Garland, Texas 75044
(972) 205-2765
www.golffirewheel.com

Greens – Champion Bermuda
Cost of Play – Mon-Thurs $$ Fri-Sun $$

Bar/Beverage Cart –

Practice Facility –

Favorite Holes
        Old Course - Hole #9, 552 Yards, Par 5
        Lakes Course – Hole #10, 414 Yards, Par 4

Old Course Grade – 🏁🏁🏁

Lakes Course Grade – 🏁🏁🏁

Overall Grade – ☆☆☆

The Bridges Course

1535 East Brand
Garland, Texas 75044
(972) 205-2795 or (972) 205-2797

www.golffirewheel.com

Greens – Bent Grass

Cost of Play – Mon-Thurs $$ Fri-Sun $$$

Bar/Beverage Cart – 🛢🛢🛢🛢🛢🛢

Practice Facility –

The Bridges is made up of 3 separate 9 hole courses. Any combination to complete an 18 hole course is covered by the course and overall grade.

Course Grade – 🏁🏁🏁🏁

Overall Grade – ☆☆☆☆☆

Favorite Hole   The Masters – Hole #3, 325 Yards, Par 4

Grapevine Golf Course

Located right behind the Lake Grapevine Dam, Grapevine Golf Course has been newly renovated by professional golfer/designer, D. A. Weibring. The first renovations since the course opened in the late 1970's, the City of Grapevine should be applauded for endeavoring to make the most of this scenic location and so generously adding to the highlights surrounding the dam.

Three distinct 9's provide a lot of options off the tee depending only on how much of a risk taker you really are. A long iron or fairway metal may well be the best choice from the tee. Most of the greens are average in size and have subtle breaks in them. Big trees, elevations changes, creative landscaping and environmental areas make variety the norm here, so expect to continuously be fully engaged. Forget about boredom, this course is clearly a step above ordinary municipal courses and therefore does not need to bear that distinction.

Here's an idea: Check yourself into Gaylord Texan and get a room overlooking the lake. Set your tee times for a few warm up games at Grapevine Golf Course. Play until you feel like you're peaking, then head right beside it to our Best Overall course, Cowboy's Golf Club. A perfect duo, together these two pack the best punch in the metroplex and make for an excellent excuse to stay on vacation.

The Godfather – Straight, crooked, short, long, twists and turns. Are you dizzy yet? I hope not, you will want to remember everything about this course. A great test of mental golf, your best chance for a good score is to stay open minded with your shot making. The only redundant part of the course are the fairly easy to putt greens.

Jodella – This course is definitely a huge step above the average and mundane municipal golf course. As with most D.A. Weibring designs, this course offers you generous fairways, a few bunkers, and relatively tame greens. The difference here lies on the Bluebonnet 9, where he cleverly used the natural landscape to make the fairways tighter. So, bring out your creative game, this course is well mixed and clearly out of the normal Weibring pattern.

The Vokster – Short hitters like me will especially enjoy the average length par 4's. I also love the wide fairways, because they enable me to spend less time looking for my ball and more time to drink beer.

Grapevine Golf Course

	Par	Yardage	Rating	Slope
Pecan/Mockingbird	72	6983	73.9	136
Mockingbird/Bluebonnet	72	6901	73.3	132
Pecan/Bluebonnet	72	7060	73.5	133

3800 Fairway Drive
Grapevine, Texas 76051
(817) 410-3377

www.ci.grapevine.tx.us.com

Greens – Tiff Eagle

Cost of Play – Mon-Thurs $$ Fri-Sun $$

Bar/Beverage Cart –

Practice Facility –

Course Grade –

Overall Grade – ★ ☆ ☆ ☆

Favorite Hole – Hole #4, 578 Yards, Par 5 – Pecan Course

KEETON PARK GOLF COURSE

Established in 1979 by the City of Dallas, this municipal course has seen very little changes. Resting in the Elm Fork flood plane of the Trinity River, it may not be a good choice after a recent rain. Course conditions are rarely very good, but the overall layout is better than most others in its' group. In the past few years, Dallas has begun to remodel and upgrade these municipals. Hopefully, they will seize on the opportunity this course provides and bring it up to its full potential.

Keeton offers two distinctly different nines. The first 6 holes of the front nine play in and amongst the trees. The remaining holes set up the transition to the back nine, where the course opens up and water seems to come into play on almost every hole creating the biggest obstacle by far. Bunkers are basically obsolete, residing only on a few holes. Greens are elevated slightly because of the flood plane, but predominantly flat and simple. The 'bump and run' shot is clearly 'the' choice around these greens.

Because it resides in a flood plane, no houses surround this course providing a measure of peace and tranquility rarely found in the city. As with all municipals, the price is right to practice your game here. So all in all, considering the conditions this course brings a good value for your dollar.

The Godfather – Keeton Park is one of the original golf courses The Goofy Golfers learned the game and basic golf etiquette on – we're still working on both of them. In fact, that is where we learned to always set the brake on the golf cart. On hole #13, The Vokster forgot to set the brake at the top of the big mound behind the green. Consequently, the golf cart wound up in the pond behind the green and it took all 4 of us to get it out. All that could be seen was about 6" of the cart top, his floating glove and cigarettes. It just so happened to be March, 49 degrees and windy. We were soaked, but dedicated golfers that we are, we finished the round. We learned the hard way that golf carts don't make good submarines.

Double R – I will always remember the day I broke 90 on this golf course. The guy that introduced me to the game gave me a four footer for par so I could shoot that splendid 89.

The Vokster – This is my kind of course! Medium length with accurate shots required – just like mine. I love a course that begs for the 'bump and run' shots. Luckily for me, most of my shots (tee, iron, etc.) look like that. I rule on this course!

Keeton Park Golf Course

	Par	Yardage	Rating	Slope
Back	72	6521	70.6	113
Middle	72	6062	68.6	113
Front	72	5054	68.1	113

2323 North Jim Miller Road
Dallas, Texas 75227
(214) 670-8784

www.keetonpark.com

Greens – Bermuda

Cost of Play – Mon-Thurs $ Fri-Sun $$

Bar/Beverage Cart

Practice Facility –

Course Grade –

Overall Grade – ✩ ✩

Favorite Hole – Hole #3, 538 Yards, Par 5

LAKE ARLINGTON GOLF COURSE

Located just below Lake Arlington Dam, this course is medium length with some tree lined fairways and wide-open holes. All the greens are fairly flat with little or no trouble around them. There are no bunkers, so leave the sand bucket and shovel at home.

Owned by the City of Arlington, this municipal course was built in 1963 and they haven't looked forward since. Planned to provide even the best hacker a fun outing, they will particularly enjoy playing from the tips. And gear is minimal. You only need one ball on this course and a Texas wedge. Beginners unite, hackers rejoice and slicers salute! This is a course only Happy Gilmore could love.

The Godfather – It's amazing what sand traps do for a golf course. Traps add another dimension to the game of golf. Unfortunately, there are no traps at Lake Arlington Golf Course, therefore the runner-up shot is a premium. Seriously though, this is a good golf course for the beginning golfer. I guess that's why Jodella and The Vokster call for a tee time every week.

Double R – With most of the Par 4's at 370 yards or less and a par 5 at 469 yards, a good score can be had here. And if your game lacks distance, it would be a perfect layout to play. This course is easy to play and easy to score on. In fact, Jodella says if you can't score on this course, you might want to think about a sex change. I don't know if I would have said that though.

Jodella – The front nine doesn't have much to offer. The back nine, particularly #11 through #14, are the four best holes on the course back to back. #14 is particularly unique with the tee box located at the top of the dam and the shot dropping 80+ feet to the green below. But that's the highlight, so be sure you enjoy it.

The Vokster – Warning, Warning, I repeat Warning: Do not try to hit the high towering tee ball here. The choice of shots should clearly be the worm burner. And after that massive tee ball, it is just another short worm burner to the green. Short hitters like me will especially enjoy the average length par 4's. Please, somebody pass me a cold beer....

Lake Arlington Golf Course

	Par	Yardage	Rating	Slope
Blue	71	6637	70.7	117
White	71	6204	68.5	111
Red	71	5485	71.0	114

1516 West Green Oaks Boulevard
Arlington, Texas 76013
(817) 451-6101

www.arlingtongolf.com

Greens – Bermuda

Cost of Play – Mon-Thurs $ Fri-Sun $

Bar/Beverage Cart – No Cans!

Practice Facility –

Course Grade –

Overall Grade –

Favorite Hole – Hole #14, 240 Yards, Par 3

LAKE PARK GOLF CLUB

Lake Park Golf Club is perfect for beginners and those who need to work on their short game. Playing within view of Lake Lewisville, the terrain is flat and trees are scarce. There are very few hazards to deal with. In fact, the biggest watch out on this track are the other golfers yelling 'Fore!'.

Most holes play adjacent to each other, so blown tee balls in adjoining fairways allow shots into the greens. And yet, despite the heavy and often unrelenting traffic in the fairways, the course stays in pretty good condition. Hey, you got to start somewhere. For you beginners, this is the perfect place to learn the game and practice your golf etiquette.

The Godfather – People that play golf at Lake Park would think The Vokster was Phil Mickleson if they saw him hit the ball. Many of the par 4's are 7 iron, 7 iron, to the middle of the green or you can change it up and hit 6 iron, 8 iron. On several tee boxes you can tee off in any direction and play a different hole. It's like customizing your own course. Well, there are some golf courses for everyone and Lake Park is for beginners and hackers.

Jodella – Not bad for a little municipal course. Playing to a par 70, at 6135 yards long, this is a great place to bring your kids, wife or any beginner and is a hackers dream come true. It is short, with flat greens, 3 or 4 bunkers, just a few hazards and excellent tee boxes. They have a good practice facility and a lighted driving range. However, I do have to highly recommend you wear a hard hat, because there are several intersections of cart paths that come together all at once. Talk about a pile up!

Little Leonard – There is not a lot of pizzazz to this course, with only 3 bunkers, and little to no water, but it is still a good little course to improve your game. Just please don't try to pick up pointers from some of the unorthodox swings you will see from other golfers on this course. That could scar you for life! But don't misunderstand, the Goofy Golfers appreciate any golf course that is well maintained, making improvements, and is still fun, no matter what the level. Hell! Not too long ago, we were there ourselves!

The Vokster – Looking for a place to get in a quick round of golf? This course is very short and easy to score on, kind of like the women back in my dating days. And remember, Jodella started on a track similar to this and now hits the ball as far as anyone I know.

Lake Park Golf Club

	Par	Yardage	Rating	Slope
Blue	70	6135	68.3	108
White	70	5740	66.5	102
Red	70	4960	N/A	N/A

6 Lake Park Road
Lewisville, Texas 75057
(972) 219-5661

www.lakeparkgc.com

Greens – Tiff Dwarf

Cost of Play – Mon-Thurs $ Fri-Sun $$

Bar/Beverage Cart –

Practice Facility –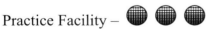

Course Grade – ⚐

Overall Grade – ☆ ☆

Favorite Hole – Hole #18, 505 Yards, Par 5

L. B. Houston Golf Course

The Dallas municipal courses have so much potential and L. B. Houston is no exception. Set in an old gravel pit, small lakes, ponds and bar ditches come into play on 13 of the 18 holes. Even though it plays like a links style, there are lines of trees down the fairways. Wooded terrain makes you forget you are in the mid Dallas area, but it begs for more attention.

L. B. Houston changes play with the weather. Spring rains cause flooding, but when the hot summer sun bakes it, the crevices and cracks appear to swallow up your ball. Any approach shot even close to the green will leave you a simple up and down for par, as there is very little trouble around the greens.

Great for those needing to stretch their legs and entertainment dollars, this course may prove to be beginners luck, but would greatly benefit from some greenbacks. Expect no frills and little thrills. This one lives up to the reputation 'munies' have so sadly earned.

The Godfather – L. B. Houston, like many other municipals, is laid in some low-lying land. Playing conditions are good at best. Maintenance on a golf course costs money, that will help you understand how much bang to expect out of a $30.00 green fee. Serious, savvy golfers need not apply.

Double R – This course has potential, but is very flat and so are the greens. Plenty of trees on both sides of the fairway make your tee shot important here. Amenities are much like the course; in serious need of upgrades.

Jodella – The front 9 is more open and a bit easier, but it also has the only greenside bunkers on it; and they're all steep faced, so make sure you avoid them. The back 9 has many more trees, with the last 5 holes smack dab in the middle of them. Trees line both sides of the fairways on these holes. Another neat thing is that 2 holes on the back have a tree or two that are actually out in the fairway and make you have to work your shot around them. This course would seriously challenge The Vokster and Double R, if they were dumb enough to forget their beer.

The Vokster – Back and forth, back and forth. Oops, that hole doglegged eight feet. Oh, *that* was the signature hole! I swear, if there wasn't any beer to drink, that wouldn't have been a challenge at all.

L. B. Houston Golf Course

	Par	Yardage	Rating	Slope
Back	72	6705	70.8	126
Middle	72	6290	69.8	120
Forward	73	5596	72.8	113

11223 Luna Road
Dallas, Texas 75229
(214) 670-6322

www.lbhoustongolf.com

Greens – Bermuda

Cost of Play – Mon-Thurs $ Fri-Sun $$

Bar/Beverage Cart –

Practice Facility –

Course Grade –

Overall Grade –

Favorite Hole – Hole #17, 545 Yards, Par 5

LEGACY RIDGE COUNTRY CLUB

Without question, the unique contrast of the two nines is the main attraction for Legacy Ridge. Designed by Bill Johnston, the front nine is a true links style with no trees, very little rough, abundant native grasses and a ton of water. The back nine winds through a pecan orchard and around a large pond. Add in the variety of greens sizes and this course may well be considered a diamond in the rough.

Be sure to stop by the clubhouse first for a clear view of the front nine before playing. It will be your last chance to plan, because once you drop the 40 feet to the course, visibility between holes decreases considerably. Perhaps the only course that actually contains a series of canals on the front nine, it introduces an interesting alternative to usual North Texas golf. Providing formidable barriers and snaking hand in hand with par robbing rough, realize early on that when your ball goes missing, you need not go looking for it.

In contrast, most of the back nine was carved right out of a large pecan orchard. Big scattered trees are generously sprinkled throughout fat fairways that roll slowly around before giving way to a levied tee box beside the pond. Basically mid length and not an overpowering or demanding course at 6750 yards, Legacy Ridge is still well worth the trip out to Bonham.

The Godfather – Do not try to choke these fairways with a deep driver off the tee or you are sure to get penalized with any errant shot. Bunkers on the course are as forgiving as they are shallow and flat; so don't expect them to explain your penalties.

Double R – The back nine should play a little easier. At least you can find your ball in the trees, instead of donating them to the fishes in the canals. Green sizes are particularly interesting. Short holes have small greens and longer holes have bigger greens. Clearly some thought went into the design, making for a fair challenge to your game.

Jodella – There is nothing I like better than a course that finishes with a par 5, because it gives you an opportunity to end with a birdie. Playing at only 480 yards long, the great silverback can't wait to tee off, but beware of your shot to the green because the large lake to the right will turn your birdie to a bogie or worse.

The Vokster – I can't decide if it is a big pond or a small lake, but I do like the pecans in my beer at Legacy Ridge.

Legacy Ridge Country Club

	Par	Yardage	Rating	Slope
Black	72	6750	72.7	131
Blue	72	6379	71.3	125
White	72	6065	69.8	125
Gold	72	5573	66.9	118
Red	72	5102	70.9	122

2201 Country Club Drive
Bonham, Texas 75418
(903) 640-4800

www.legacyridge.com

Greens – Bent Grass

Cost of Play – Mon-Thurs $$ Fri-Sun $$

Bar/Beverage Cart –

Practice Facility –

Course Grade –

Overall Grade –

Favorite Hole – Hole #12, 416 Yards, Par 4

LOS RIOS COUNTRY CLUB

A semi-private club that offers memberships to everyone, it is also open for public play. Originally set up with a country club atmosphere, the overall facility is surrounded by amenities including a clubhouse, tennis courts and a swimming pool, but only the golf course is available to the public.

Built in the lowlands around a fairly large creek, the golf course at Los Rios has long since lost its luster. The rainy season in Texas wreaks havoc on this course, alternating between mud and dried out flats. With a dependency on good weather, even when conditions are at their best, this course does not live up to the stellar reputation Plano enjoys overall.

Created in the early 1970's by noted golfer, Don January, it premiered as a top-notch course, but has enjoyed few changes over time. The course is in good conditions, greens are well bunkered, doglegs are challenging and water holes are reasonably placed, making this a decent test of golf on a rather short course.

The Godfather – Do not play Los Rio during extreme weather conditions. Until ownership adds dollars to the improvement budget, Los Rios remains on my 'don't need to play list'.

Little Leonard – Los Rios is flat as a pancake and short to boot! It is not demanding off the tee, so good iron players can take advantage of the short length. Once on the fairly flat greens, putting is not too difficult. If only the women were that easy.

The Vokster – The practice facility is rather small by today's standards, but is conveniently located near the first tee box. This short track should leave you feeling like your game is improving. Finish up the day with a drink in the clubhouse or plan to eat dinner as you watch the sun go down. Those wanting to linger into the night might pack a deck of cards. Who knows, you might just earn back your green fees.

Los Rios Country Club

	Par	Yardage	Rating	Slope
Blue	71	6507	70.1	127
White	71	6102	70.0	119
Red	71	5076	72.2	122

1700 Country Club Drive
Plano, Texas 75074
(972) 424-4546

www.irigolfgroup.com

Greens – Bermuda

Cost of Play – Mon-Thurs $$ Fri-Sun $$

Bar/Beverage Cart –

Practice Facility –

Course Grade –

Overall Grade –

Favorite Hole – Hole #14, 493 Yards, Par 5

MESQUITE GOLF COURSE

This city owned course is reasonably priced, but could definitely benefit from a huge infusion of money. Talk about low hanging fruit! The City of Mesquite could begin anywhere and make a sizable improvement. Land on this course is abundant enough to update and modernize, but until that happens, it doesn't take much imagination to realize this one is at the bottom of the list.

Want to learn the game and don't have the appropriate clubs or clothing? Jeans and tennis shoes are in order here and no one keeps tabs on your etiquette. Beginners beware, even when you master the grass, you still don't have much to brag about. Bring the kids, but don't bring the boss!

The Godfather – There is not a whole lot you can say that is positive about Mesquite Golf Course. It is a great place to practice your un-sharpened skills. With that being said, it goes hand in hand that you will see all types of golfers. With no real dress code enforced, there is as much variation and color here as a night at the Grammy's.

Double R – If you are thinking about quitting the game of golf, then come play this course because it will help speed up the process.

Jodella – Bring a tote sack when you play here. Because when you hit a ball in the creek, you can stoop to pick up aluminum cans for a little extra cash on the way home. The longer the book, the farther down the list this one goes. It easily has the distinction of always coming in dead last.

The Vokster – Very little doglegs and no traps! Par 5's are all reachable in 2! So, if any of those things pose a problem in your game, worry no more at Mesquite's public course. It is easy on the wallet and the mind. With flat redundant holes that run back and forth like a Six Flags line, the only true hazard out here is the absence of a bar.

Mesquite Golf Course

	Par	Yardage	Rating	Slope
Back	71	6280	69.1	116
Middle	71	5933	67.3	112
Forward	72	5153	67.4	112

825 North Highway 67
Mesquite, Texas 75150
(972) 270-7457

www.americangolf.com

Greens – Bermuda

Cost of Play – Mon-Thurs $ Fri-Sun $$

Bar/Beverage Cart –

Practice Facility –

Course Grade –

Overall Grade – ☆

Favorite Hole – Hole #13, 153 Yards, Par 3

OAK HOLLOW GOLF COURSE

It is great to see any golf course adding amenities to their facility, especially those with obvious possibilities. Oak Hollow has always been known for the open layout, but eventually that will change. In 1998, the course was redesigned and over 300 trees were added to force play in each individual fairway. Over time, they are expected to tighten up the course considerably. Oak Hollow is definitely headed in the right direction even if it will take a few years to reach their full capabilities.

The length at Oak Hollow is 6679 yards from the back tees and has only two par 5's. While it may appear on the short side, it does actually have championship length because it is a par 70 track. However, with few sand traps, slight elevation changes and a few average water hazards, it still remains a beginner or novice course.

Fun, fair, slightly challenging and a good value, the City of McKinney has created a pleasant diversion for weekend golfers. In an area with plentiful courses to choose from, it certainly provides an accommodating start to a life long sport.

The Godfather – Many municipals allow adjoining fairway play, but thanks to strategically placed trees, golfers looking to "cheese up" the course can no longer do that. More municipals need to take notice of Oak Hollow. Obviously millions of dollars are not required to make substantial changes.

Jodella – You'll do well to have a lot of birdie putts on these postage stamp greens. The signature hole #8, a par 4, 421 yards long, borders on the unfair making it perfect for The Goofy Golfers. The harder the hole, the more we like it. Hey, maybe we can play this hole 18 times!

The Vokster – What once was Ma and Pa Kettle's 9-hole goat ranch is now a decent 18-hole golf course. In addition to more trees, they've added 5 new bunkers, dwarf bermuda greens, a new cart barn, pavilion and most importantly, a liquor license! You'll be pleasantly surprised by this course.

Oak Hollow Golf Course

	Par	Yardage	Rating	Slope
Blue	70	6679	72.3	121
White	70	6077	69.2	118
Red	70	5080	68.8	115

3005 North McDonald Street, #5
McKinney, Texas 75071
(972) 562-0670

www.oakhollow.com

Greens – Dwarf Bermuda

Cost of Play – Mon-Thurs $ Fri-Sun $$

Bar/Beverage Cart –

Practice Facility –

Course Grade – ⚑ ⚑

Overall Grade – ☆ ☆

Favorite Hole – Hole #8, 421 Yards, Par 4

OLD BRICKYARD GOLF COURSE

If you are a golfer and love roller coasters, travel 20 minutes south of downtown Dallas to the Old Brickyard Golf Course. You must be at least 48" tall and remember to keep your arms and legs in your cart at all times. Clubs and other loose objects are not the responsibility of the Old Brickyard if lost. All joking aside, this golf course offers something that few others in the area can boast about: dramatic elevation change.

For you "Bombin' Bettys" out there, you may want to think about leaving the driver in the bag. Because from the tips, the course only plays to 6486 yards with a total par of 71. But don't let the short yardage fool you; this can still be a very challenging course. The smart play off the tee is a long iron or fairway wood. If you must hit the driver, then this becomes a risk/reward type course. However, if you take too many risks, you may finish the day feeling like you have bricks for brains.

The Godfather – The Brickyard is more different than any course in the area, because they had so little land to work with. Several holes are divided by sheer wall cliffs that a billy goat would have trouble clinging to. Now don't get me wrong, the cliffs range from about 20 to 50 feet tall, but they are very vertical. Long irons are fine off the tee because this track is short. So, don't get greedy off the tee or your ball will end up being goat food.

Double R - This unique course borders I-45 just south of Dallas, which explains the huge net that divides I-45 from the driving range, to keep you from imbedding your ball in someone's windshield. A lot of tricked up shots will keep you guessing and this course will never be boring!

Jodella - Every hole on the front nine is completely different and fun. But after the tenth hole, play quickly becomes average. You don't need a driver on this course. That should be good right? Not! Because I have to hit long irons instead of drivers, I remain eternally confused and can always expect to come in last on the score. I much prefer facing an angry commuter with a golf ball size ding in his hood.

The Vokster – One of the most enjoyable low budget courses in the Metroplex. With lots of dunes and elevation changes, you're sure to enjoy it. And if your competition happens to be beating you, Old Brickyard supplies plenty of bricks to beanpole them with.

Old Brickyard Golf Course

	Par	Yardage	Rating	Slope
Gold	71	6486	70.6	125
Blue	71	6056	68.6	119
White	71	4611	62.5	102

605 North I-45
Ferris, Texas 75125
(972) 842-8700

www.oldbrickyardgolf.com

Greens – Tiff Eagle

Cost of Play – Mon-Thurs $$ Fri-Sun $$

Bar/Beverage Cart –

Practice Facility –

Course Grade –

Overall Grade – ☆ ☆ ☆

Favorite Hole – Hole #10, 553 Yards, Par 5

Pecan Hollow Golf Course

Built in the mirror image of Los Rios around Rowlett Creek, Pecan Hollow is designed by the team of Don January and Billy Martindale. Now enjoying recent improvements to the clubhouse, proshop and grill/bar, the facilities are better, but the course remains a very bland layout in poor repair.

Catering to the high handicap golfer looking for a deal on fees, the potential is there, but sadly plans are not in the works for major course renovations. It is a shame the City of Plano does not take notice of other cities, who have realized the value of updating their courses more effectively.

What a great piece of property to build a golf course on! Huge, old trees and two creeks coming into play all in one place. Plano, can you say, "Hello opportunity"? Wake up and hear the screaming of serious golfers, this one begs for a reprieve from mediocrity.

The Godfather – Back and forth, up and down. Very easy to figure out there wasn't a problem being over budget when this track was constructed. In fact, the contractor may have put a few of those budget dollars in his own pocket. Inadequate draining which in turn takes its toll on the conditions of the course, makes this only a good place for beginning golfers to practice their skills. If you never get a chance to play Pecan Hollow, I don't think you need to cry about it. On the other hand, Plano did spend big bucks on their new clubhouse. So in all fairness, I guess that does give golfers a great place to talk about what a crummy golf course they just played.

Double R – Don't worry about losing too many balls out here, the real trouble – Rowlett Creek and the trees – only come into play on a few holes. If you spray a little off the tee box, few penalties will be had. Greens are easy and with little bunkering, even the short game hacks will enjoy this track.

Jodella – When you first start to play golf and come to a place like Pecan Hollow, you don't know any different. When it was originally built and there was not much to compare to, it shone like a diamond. With the growth and advancements of courses all over the metroplex, the shine has slowly but surely been reduced to an old chunk of coal.

The Vokster – Why did Plano improve the 19th hole and not the golf course? I'll never tell. All I can say is, Bud Light sent me a personal thank you note. And boys, you're always welcome.

<u>Pecan Hollow Golf Course</u>

	Par	Yardage	Rating	Slope
Blue	72	6772	70.1	115
White	72	6231	68.1	110
Senior	72	5870	71.3	118
Ladies	72	5320	66.1	105

4501 East 14th Street
Plano, Texas 75074
(972) 941-7600

No Website Available

Greens – Bermuda

Cost of Play – Mon-Thurs $$ Fri-Sun $$

Bar/Beverage Cart –

Practice Facility –

Course Grade –

Overall Grade – ☆ ☆ ☆

Favorite Hole – Hole #11, 519 Yards, Par 5

PLANTATION GOLF CLUB

Short, open and easy to play, this is an average golfers paradise. Playing at just 6402 yards, you'll never be overwhelmed by the length. The driver is not a requirement off the tee; however, any errant shot could be penalized, as there is OB on almost every hole. After a good tee ball, short irons are the norm. If you love to hit wedges, look no further than Plantation.

Generally par 4's are the hardest part of any course, but with only two par fours playing over 400 yards, these are much easier than the norm. Predominantly flat, a level stance will make all your shots easier. Average golfers known to slice a ball occasionally will probably become well acquainted with the out-of-bounds (OB).

Water in front of the greens on the short par 4's makes the play more interesting. The par 5's are all reachable in 2 and the longest par 3 is 188 yards. Greens are average in size, flat without a lot of undulation and putting should be easy. In other words, it's easier to score here than it is to get under a southern belles hoop skirt!

The Godfather – When you go to the driving range in preparation for your play here, all you need are the wedges in your bag. If you love to brag and exaggerate about what a great golfer you are then this is your place. Sadly, Plantation is about as challenging as The Godfather coming home with pretty girls' phone numbers from the local bars.

Double R – If you can't hit your driver, or don't own one, this is your course. Short gamers will appreciate the opportunity to exercise their biceps at the great bar and grill. The Vokster's handicap is always the lowest there!

Jodella – Don't come to Plantation expecting ante bellum homes and sprawling acreage. This course is surrounded by houses on small lots and less than pristine landscaping. In my opinion, the only sport on this course is trying to catch a glimpse of women taking showers through the house windows.

The Vokster – If you keep your ball in play, no problems! But if you hit out of bounds, you better hope you miss the windows. Jodella has met many of the homeowners like that!

Plantation Golf Club

	Par	Yardage	Rating	Slope
Back	72	6402	70.9	122
Middle	72	5945	68.1	117
Forward	72	4916	70.4	113

4701 Plantation Lane
Frisco, Texas 75035
(972) 335-4653

www.plantationgolf.net

Greens – Champion Bermuda

Cost of Play – Mon-Thurs $$ Fri-Sun $$

Bar/Beverage Cart –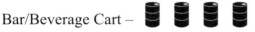

Practice Facility –

Course Grade – 🚩🚩🚩

Overall Grade – ☆☆☆

Favorite Hole – Hole #18, 386 Yards, Par 4

Prairie Lakes Golf Course

Prairie Lakes Golf Club used to be the old Grand Prairie Municipal. It was established in 1965 and originally designed by Ralph Plummer. The golf course consists of 3 nines: The Red, The White and The Blue. The Red Course recently completed extensive renovations and reopened in late 2004. The other two nines will be individually renovated over the next two years, but 18 holes will always be available for play. Greens will be changed to Champion Bermuda and some holes will be lengthened. Also expect some greens and tee boxes to be totally repositioned.

Calm, peaceful and beautiful, this city golf course affords a real country feel. Several holes play right on the banks of Eagle Mountain Lake. Eventually, 15 of the 27 holes will have some type of water hazard to contend with and almost every fairway will be lined with native trees. Pampas grass is plentiful and provides a crisp, picturesque flavor anyone can enjoy.

Despite bearing the distinction of a municipal course, Prairie Lakes has a country club feel. It is surprisingly clean and access to plentiful water will continue to keep it in very serviceable condition. Easy to play, the rough is short and bunkers do not exist. Greens are oddly shaped and enjoy subtle mounding. An awesome combination for the average golfer, Prairie Lakes is reasonably priced and provides a very pleasurable golfing experience.

Double R – Short in length, Prairie Lakes is a fun course to play. Good accurate tee shots here will leave you with some flip wedges to the green and a good opportunity to go low. If you're looking to set a personal best score, this may well be your track.

Jodella – I was really impressed with the Par 3's out here. Every Par 3 except for one is 190 yards or longer and incorporates some type of water hazard in front of the green. The Godfather likes that it is so easy to walk. That way, he gets to ride alone and enjoy a little peace.

The Vokster – I'm always happy to play a short course with a little low bump and run chip shot. My only concern is this 27-hole layout. Do I get to bring a cooler and a half? I'll never be totally happy until they put a major refueling spot in the middle.

Prairie Lakes Golf Course

Red Course

	Par	Yardage	Rating
Back	36	3340	35.5
Middle	36	3095	34.1
Front	36	2416	32.6

White Course

	Par	Yardage	Rating	Slope
Back	35	3014	34.0	54
Middle	35	2802	32.9	51
Front	35	2478	31.6	47

Blue Course

	Par	Yardage	Rating	Slope
Back	36	3308	35.5	58
Middle	36	3084	34.4	56
Front	36	2775	32.7	51

3202 Southeast 14th Street
Grand Prairie, Texas 75052
(972) 263-0661

www.prairielakesgolf.com

Greens – Champion Bermuda

Cost of Play – Mon-Thurs $ Fri-Sun $

Bar/Beverage Cart –

Practice Facility –

Course Grade – ⚑ ⚑ ⚑

Overall Grade – ☆ ☆ ☆

Favorite Hole – (White Course) Hole #6, 372 Yards, Par 4

Red Oak Valley Golf Club

Hello Hackers! Want to try your game against a train? At Red Oak Valley, you can play alongside and over the tracks. Be sure to designate at least one person to listen for the train whistle or this could become a serious challenge.

Red Oak is at the top of the 'don't even think about it list'. Basically an overrated cow pasture, it is just a cut above your own back yard. The only good mounding on the course was put in by the local fire ants. With no apparent changes in sight, this one is actually best thought of as a last resort.

Talk about begging for either renovation or closure! We feel the only 'right' this course should experience is 'last rites'. No hazards, no sand traps and no pressure, if you are just starting the game, you can be a hero in your own eyes here.

The Godfather – In a race with only a few contenders, this nag is jockeying for last place. Fairways are wide open, so open, in fact, single engine planes may mistake them for landing strips. The greens are unelevated and stay in great shape thanks to the thousands of worms that reside there. Unfortunately, the left over worm castings give whole new meaning to the word hazard. Can you say worm putt?

Double R – This course is short in length playing at 5911 yards. If you like the 'bump and run' shot or don't have a full set of clubs, this is your course. Short knockers rejoice – this is your Mecca!

Jodella – This one may well have the designation of the smallest greens in the metroplex. Some of my ex-girlfriends have had bigger butts than most of these greens. And they were more interesting, too.

Little Leonard – With all the grass cut the same length (greens, fairways, and rough), and very short par 4's, if you are on the green, make the putt for eagle. If you are not on the green, make the putt for eagle. And watch out for the railroad tracks that come into play. If you land your ball on the tracks you might find a "Choo-Choo" running up your caboose!

Red Oak Valley Golf Club

	Par	Yardage	Rating	Slope
Men	70	5911	N/A	N/A
Ladies	72	5911	N/A	N/A

Rural Route #5
Red Oak, Texas 75154
(972) 617-3249

No Web Address

Greens – Bermuda

Cost of Play – Mon-Thurs $ Fri-Sun $

Bar/Beverage Cart –

Practice Facility –

Course Grade – ⚑

Overall Grade – ☆

Favorite Hole – Hole #10, 427 Yards, Par 4

Ridgeview Ranch Golf Club

We love Jeff Brauer designs because we can always count on excellent use of fairway traps and awesome greens. At Ridgeview Ranch, the combination of a Brauer design and American Golf ownership truly makes for a wonderful place to play. With length reaching over 7,000 yards and trouble on most every hole, those shooting a low score here can really consider it an accomplishment.

Variety is the spice of life at Ridgeview Ranch. Creeks, OB, wide fairways, tight fairways, elevated greens, mounding and good bunkering makes for a great mixture of holes and plenty of trouble. Smart golfers will do well to take advantage of the shorter front nine and save extra strokes for the more demanding finish.

Missing only the desired elevation and tight play that makes the top courses tougher, Plano can be proud of this reasonably priced course. Come prepared to use every club in your bag and test your skills. There's a whole lot to love about Ridgeview Ranch.

The Godfather – Don't let your playing buddies screw with your mind here. You really need to stay focused. Hit the ball to the largest part of the fairway, even if it leaves you a longer approach shot. This is a great course to try talking your buddies into hitting the driver if they are stupid enough to fall for an old trick.

Double R – This course has some elevation changes from tee to green that are just beautiful. On the back, you are in for a fight with the par 5 at 570, par 4 at 482, and par 3 at 220 yards. These three holes are about the toughest stretch of holes around. If they beat you up too bad, go meet The Vokster at the bar for a cold one. Tell him I sent you.

Jodella – The 4 par 3's on this course are really quite different. For example, #5 is 149 yards, #7 is 161 yards, #17 is 193 yards and #12's 220 yards are protected by 6 bunkers! That's the reason Jeff Brauer rules! He lulls you to sleep, then wakes you up with the shotgun approach. This is definitely a course where Double R and The Vokster will be crying in their beer, but that's no problem as long as I'm not buying.

The Vokster – If it's true that practice makes perfect, Ridgeview surely has that covered. Their putting green, practice bunker and driving range are great ways to improve your skills. Of course, my favorite hole at Ridgeview Ranch is the 19th one. With a wonderful bar and grill, should your game begin to suffer you will have no trouble answering to the call of the beer babes. At least it's never been a problem for me!

Ridgeview Ranch Golf Club

	Par	Yardage	Rating	Slope
Copper	72	7025	74.1	130
Blue	72	6529	71.8	125
White	72	6135	70.0	120
Silver	72	5335	70.4	117

2701 Ridgeview Drive
Plano, Texas 75025
(972) 390-1039

no website

Greens – Champion Bermuda

Cost of Play – Mon-Thurs $$ Fri-Sun $$

Bar/Beverage Cart –

Practice Facility –

Course Grade – 🚩🚩🚩🚩

Overall Grade – ★★★★

Favorite Hole – Hole #4, 347 Yards, Par 4

119

Riverchase Golf Club

Riverchase Golf Club in Coppell is owned and managed by American Golf. Generally speaking, that means they enjoy regular maintenance and remain in good condition. Open with minimal trees, this course appears almost simple, but the test here lies in the OB and water. Don't misunderstand, room is still available and only hookers and slicers will find trouble. After all, thirteen of the 18 holes have out of bounds on the left and 12 holes have water on the right. In other words, only straight hitters will prevail.

Short in terms of yardage, a good game still remains and will keep your attention. Greens are elevated, two-tiered and average with moderate undulation lending themselves to deep bunkers. With exception of #10 and #18, all holes are straight on. No 'forced carries' are necessary as the fronts of the greens are totally unprotected.

Bring the boss to play this course and then make a lasting impression at the Cowboy's Sports Café Bar and Grill, just about 2 miles south of Riverchase on MacArthur Boulevard. Tell the owner The Goofy Golfers sent you and order a plate of his famous hot wings. Golf, football, wings, beautiful servers and beer.... Hey, this calls for an instant replay.

The Godfather – The whole front nine on this course borders a residential area, so if you hook the ball and I mean really hook it, you may want to take out some broken window insurance. Unless you are like The Godfather and are looking for an excuse to meet new people... ...er, women.

Double R – The first time I played golf with Jodella was at Riverchase. He birdied the first two holes and I was really impressed. The only thing he has done since to impress me was join a fitness club to carve down his famous physique, of course the jury is still out on that....

Little Leonard – Watch out for the backyard picnics at Riverchase. If the dude grillin' the burgers is not a golf fan, there could be some serious trouble. Other than that, just avoid the trouble and bang away!

The Vokster – Do your shots fly straight, short and sometimes a little thin like mine do? Do those low running flag hunters keep you going to the cooler a little too often? You are sure to drink less and score better here. Hello good score, goodbye beer. Nah! I don't think any golf game is worth that.

Riverchase Golf Club

	Par	Yardage	Rating	Slope
Back	71	6593	72.0	124
Middle	71	6041	68.9	114
Forward	71	5125	70.5	119

700 Riverchase Drive
Coppell, Texas 75019
(972) 462-8281

no website

Greens – Champion Bermuda

Cost of Play – Mon-Thurs $$ Fri-Sun $$

Bar/Beverage Cart –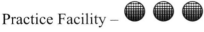

Practice Facility –

Course Grade –

Overall Grade – ☆ ☆ ☆

Favorite Hole – Hole #10, 394 Yards, Par 4

Riverside Golf Club

It doesn't matter if you just stepped off a plane at DFW or if you live in the Dallas/Fort Worth metroplex, Riverside is quick and easy to get to. Recently purchased by American Golf, they can boast about many improvements on the course and a renewed reputation.

Riverside gets its name because it sits along the banks of the Trinity River and holds true to "links style" golf, with few trees and plenty of water. In fact, water comes into play on thirteen of the eighteen holes, so be sure to bring a lot of floating golf balls, or a cane pole and minnows, depending on which sport you are interested in for the day.

Finding the fairways at Riverside is easy; hitting the greens is not. Small, narrow and well protected, they are consistently hard to hit. Together, the combination makes Riverside one of the better golfing values in the Metroplex.

The Godfather – This is one difficult layout. The par fours are long, turning, watery, to small greens. In fact, the layout is so good, if they pumped some maintenance dollars into the course, they could at least hold a qualifying tournament here. There is not that much rough, but that may be because there are so many water hazards since the course lies in the bottom of the Trinity River.

Jodella – Water, water everywhere, but not a drop to drink. That's what you'll be saying when you play this course. The Goofy Golfers love this place because we always come out of here with extra balls when we retrieve ours.

Little Leonard – Most of the greens are relatively small, with one exception: Holes #13 and #18 share the same green. I have no trouble hitting this green. It's just a shame I am always closer to the wrong hole. Now that I'm 150 feet away with my putter, the term twist and shout has a whole new meaning.

The Vokster – We used to play this course out of canoes! Where do you think The Goofy Golfers got their idea to dress in knickers anyway? That's right! Years ago, the knickers look was born, right here when the course flooded and some yo-yo rolled up his pants!

Riverside Golf Club

	Par	Yardage	Rating	Slope
Championship	72	7025	74.4	132
Back	72	6433	71.5	126
Middle	72	5785	68.4	119
Forward	72	5175	69.5	113

3000 Riverside Parkway
Grand Prairie, Texas 75050
(817) 640-7800

no website

Greens – Champion Bermuda

Cost of Play – Mon-Thurs $$ Fri-Sun $$

Bar/Beverage Cart –

Practice Facility –

Course Grade –

Overall Grade –

Favorite Hole – Hole #7, 434 Yards, Par 4

SHERRILL PARK GOLF COURSE

Richardson owns this municipal course. Opened in 1972, back in the old days golfers would show up an hour before first light to get their ball in the sleeve for a tee time. Things have changed though and so has this course. Today tee times can be scheduled by phone days in advance and old style golf is a thing of the past. Redesigned by D. A. Weibring in the late 1990's, the second 18 is now a shotmaker's course. In fact, the only thing that hasn't changed here are the snack stealing squirrels.

There are two eighteen-hole courses at Sherrill Park. Course One is 6900 yards long with subtle doglegs winding among wide, occasionally tree-lined fairways. 'Big Bombers' should enjoy playing this layout. Scattered traps and isolated water hazards will make low scores highly likely.

Course Two is 6375 yards. A Par 70 with only 2 Par 5's, it plays shorter, but more water provides heightened trouble. Fairway wood lovers and long iron players can take advantage of the shorter length. 'Hit the ball where you can see it' applies here! Target golf is required off the tee boxes and to the greens.

At Sherrill Park, pick the course that fits your game. Either way you can't lose. Both provide good value and run the gamut on perfecting your golfing skills.

The Godfather – Sherrill Park was the home course for Little Leonard and The Godfather when we first took up the game. I like Course Two best because it requires a sharp mental game to beat the tricky little traps and small ponds. All it needs is a little more yardage. And nobody knows better than The Godfather how impressive a little more yardage can be.

Jodella – On Course One, they took out trees to make it more hacker friendly and shot shaping is no longer as necessary. Don't let the short yardage on Course Two fool you, this is one tough little brute. Much like The Vokster when you try to take away his beer. Those pesky squirrels never had a chance against him.

The Vokster – The squirrels here are as bothersome as The Godfather. That little thief has been a pain in my cooler for years. I think there is a hefty padlock in my future….. I can see it now, 'Thieves 0, Vokster 12 pack'. And the crowd goes wild!

Sherrill Park Golf Course

NUMBER ONE COURSE

	Par	Yardage	Rating	Slope
Pro	72	6905	72.0	129
Championship	72	6431	71.0	124
Men	72	5832	70.0	122
Ladies	72	5181	70.0	120

NUMBER TWO COURSE

	Par	Yardage	Rating	Slope
Pro	70	6375	NA	NA
Championship	70	5934	NA	NA
Men	70	5573	NA	NA
Ladies	70	4810	NA	NA

2001 East Lookout Drive
Richardson, Texas 75082
(972) 234-1416

www.sherrillparkgolf.com

Greens – Nunber 1 Course - Tiff Dwarf   Number 2 Course - Tiff Eagle

Cost of Play – Mon-Thurs $$ Fri-Sun $$

Bar/Beverage Cart –

Practice Facility –

Course Grade for both –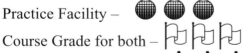

Overall Grade for both –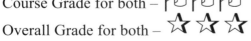

Favorite Hole:

       Number One Course - Hole #2, 385 Yards, Par 4

       Number Two Course – Hole #17, 323 Yards, Par 4

STEVENS PARK GOLF COURSE

Tradition greets you at the entrance of Stevens Park and will follow you right through the 18th hole. Centrally located in Dallas, this course was originally opened in 1924. Arthur Davis was hired to redesign it in 1983 and since that time, only the trees have continued to add to the hallowed ground. In fact, trees are more of a factor here than on any other public golf course in Dallas. Massive trunks and huge canopy's form natural shoots to the fairways and greens, creating a tricked up track that offers an opportunity to play with no woods and a bag full of irons.

Don't think you want to play a 6000 yard course? Think again! Stevens Park will have you scratching your head and praying for the 'golf gods' to find favor with your scorecard. Greens are extremely small, doglegs are severe and the creek seems constantly present. Planning is critical here, so take the time to drive it before you play.

Stevens Park is also a great place for junior golfers, to test their game. Everyone can play from the tips together and evenly compete with each other. Just plain fun, the demands of golf are all too clear at this true target course. And in our opinion, you just can't call yourself a real golfer until you've experienced all it has to offer.

Double R – If you have a bad mental game, stay away from here. Hey Jodella! Is that why you don't like to play here? Stevens Park offers one of the best mental tests of any course in the area.

Jodella – I love to play golf, but every time I tee up here I wish I never started the game. Without a doubt, this course demands smart golf. Which is exactly why I don't have a snowball's chance in hell.

Little Leonard – Better players will have to play smart and be patient or they will find their scores all shot up! Just like Texas' most infamous gangsters, Bonnie and Clyde, who hid out on this property while running from Texas Rangers.

The Vokster – What a whirlwind of a ride this one is. Tighten up the chinstraps, secure the cooler and hold on. If this one doesn't leave you with a smile on your face, you ain't breathing.

<u>Stevens Park Golf Course</u>

	Par	Yardage	Rating	Slope
Blue	71	6005	69.2	120
White	71	5544	68.5	114
Red	71	5007	68.0	118

1005 North Montclair Avenue
Dallas, Texas 75208
(214) 670-7506

www.golfindallas.net

Greens – Bermuda

Cost of Play – Mon-Thurs $ Fri-Sun $$

Bar/Beverage Cart –

Practice Facility –

Course Grade –

Overall Grade –

Favorite Hole – Hole #13, 288 Yards, Par 4

TANGLE RIDGE GOLF CLUB

Unique to the Dallas area, this course has a lot of elevation changes and rolling terrain. Located just south of Dallas, Tangle Ridge sits atop a large ridge near Joe Pool Lake, although the lake never comes into play. The fairways are plenty wide with generous landing areas, allowing for a little miscue off the tee. There are only a few water hazards to deal with, but the rough is generally thicker and taller here than on most other public courses.

From the fairways, the greens are as large as they appear. But beware of the bunkers! Deeper than most, these par robbers can cost you some strokes. Once on the greens, putting can be tricky. With big greens, boasting multiple levels and back to front slope, try to keep your approach shots below the hole or two putting will be difficult.

On a clear day, spectacular views can be had from some of the tee boxes. Enjoy the view, but keep your head in the game. Tangle Ridge was designed by the much respected Jeff Brauer. Well known for his thought provoking challenges, his designs will test your course management and make golfing fun.

Double R – The unique thing about this course is the par 5's. Three have elevated tees; so after hitting the perfect tee shot you will be left with many options. You can gamble and go for it or lay up and play it safe. No matter what choice you make, it won't be easy to do. But as they say in Texas, even a blind hog can find an acorn. I'm living proof, because this is where I made my first and only hole in one!

Jodella – Number 8 is their signature hole and also has the number one handicap rating. Playing at 575 yards uphill, it is truly a 3 shot par 5. If that's not hard enough, you must play into a prevailing south wind and cross a creek twice! Walk off with a par here and go home with 'The Official Goofy Golfers Golden Blessing.'

The Vokster – When I play this course I always bring an extra bungee cord so the beer cooler won't slide out. It's not a big thing, but I consider it critical to my game.

Tangle Ridge Golf Club

	Par	Yardage	Rating	Slope
Gold	72	6835	72.2	129
Blue	72	6337	69.9	123
White	72	5969	67.9	118
Red	72	5187	70.2	117

818 Tangle Ridge Drive
Grand Prairie, Texas 75052
(972) 299-6837

www.tangleridge.com

Greens – Bent Grass

Cost of Play – Mon-Thurs $$ Fri-Sun $$$

Bar/Beverage Cart –

Practice Facility –

Course Grade –

Overall Grade –

Favorite Hole – Hole #8, 575 Yards, Par 5

The Golf Club At Twin Creeks

Aptly named, two well-defined creeks are used on this Arnold Palmer design in Allen, Texas. A timely, yet brief renovation in the summer of 2004 changed the bent grass greens to championship Bermuda. However, the overall affect remains the same with wide-open spaces and very little rough offering a great opportunity for better than average scores.

Clean steep banks lined with large overhanging trees join up with rocky creek beds early on and it is the trees, not the creek, that require attention. Wise golfers will choose to use the generous fairways and landing areas on the first seven holes as a warm up. Hole number 8 is the most troublesome of the front nine. The back nine presents the most difficult part of the entire track while managing to keep the spacious feeling intact.

Well kept, this course is particularly attractive for any novice or average golfer. Low scores are the norm and it provides a perfect place for those with less control to improve their game. Scratch golfers should come prepared to shoot your career best.

Double R – This course has medium length at a little over 6,800 yards from the tips allowing for good scores. However, holes 15 through 18 have ruined many a good round and errant shots are abundant. 'Hikers and Bikers' may want to turn around at Hole #14 or become 'Runners and Racers'.

Little Leonard – This course could have been so much better if Arnie and his buddies weren't worried about future money to be made from the course. Two beautiful creeks run through it, but Arnold did not use them to their full potential. He kept the fairways hundreds of yards away from the creeks to allow for the "Hike and Bike" trails of future homeowners. He even put in a huge lake on hole #8 so that the commercial property at the top of the hill would bring in more money!

The Vokster – If you like to "Let the big dog eat", feast away. Yes sir, even Jodella can hardly lose a ball out here. If you favor the big stick, this one allows you to have a love affair with your driver. The last time I saw something this wide open was watching Jodella and Double R's mouths getting ready for Thanksgiving dinner!

The Golf Club At Twin Creeks

	Par	Yardage	Rating	Slope
Gold	72	6840	73.0	135
Blue	72	6288	70.5	127
White	72	5651	67.5	115
Red	72	4602	66.5	107

501 Twin Creeks Drive
Allen, Texas 75013
(972) 390-8888

www.TwinCreeksGolfClub.com

Greens – Champion Bermuda

Cost of Play – Mon-Thurs $$ Fri-Sun $$$

Bar/Beverage Cart –

Practice Facility –

Course Grade – ⚑⚑⚑

Overall Grade – ☆☆☆☆

Favorite Hole – Hole #17, 413 Yards, Par 4

THE PINNACLE CLUB

Take Hwy 175 southeast to Cedar Creek Lake for a different kind of golf course. The Pinnacle is not an easy place to find, but is well worth the search. Your ball may not be easy to find either. Playing through some of the tightest tree-lined fairways imaginable, use caution especially in the fall, lest you become knee deep in leaves.

One of the toughest short courses you will ever play, regardless of the season most greens cannot be seen from the tee box. That means almost every hole has some type of dogleg. In this shot makers dream world, your tee ball has to be on the correct side of the fairway or you are screwed. So do yourself a favor and aim to the outside bend of the doglegs to get your best shot back into the green. Greens are not overly protected and any good approach shot hit to the middle will leave you with a decent birdie putt.

Between fishing, boating, skiing and golfing, this location is an outdoor paradise. Do yourself a favor and plan to spend more than just an afternoon. Take all your outdoor equipment and use this great course as an excuse to make it a weekend getaway.

The Godfather – The Pinnacle is another think style golf course that tests your ball placement skills and patience. Irons are the game here and advancing the ball from those scrubby fairway edges is key. I have a huge advantage at a think style course with The Goofy Golfers, because The Vokster, Double R, and Jodella think about as good as they lose weight.

Jodella – My best advice here is to leave the driver in the bag, or replace one of your clubs with an axe! The fairways are a little thin, but that is because of the sandy soil. Still, it is a really fun course to play, and challenging enough to keep it interesting.

Little Leonard – This course holds a special place in my heart. The only hole in one of my golfing career was made on the second hole. Unfortunately, that shot did not hold up to the rest of my round, a smooth 101. Triumph to tragedy – a golfer's nightmare. I love this game!

The Vokster – I love to take Jodella and The Godfather here because they bitch so much about the thin lies, very soon into the round their mental games are shot. My low hot iron shots should make me the new sheriff in town. Welcome to Voksterville, home of the concrete fairway.

The Pinnacle Club

	Par	Yardage	Rating	Slope
Blue	72	6349	71.8	132
White	72	5850	69.5	126
Red	72	5116	71.2	131

200 Pinnacle Club Drive
Mabank, Texas 75156
(903) 451-9797

www.pinnaclegolfclub.com

Greens – Bermuda

Cost of Play – Mon-Thurs $$ Fri-Sun $$

Bar/Beverage Cart –

Practice Facility –

Course Grade –

Overall Grade – ☆ ☆ ☆

Favorite Hole – Hole #16, 494 Yards, Par 5

The Shores Country Club

Opened in the mid 1970's, The Shores Country Club is located along the windy shores of Lake Ray Hubbard. Initially it was set in a mostly unpopulated area. More recently it is beyond prime and could use a major refurbishing to attract the serious golfers in and around prestigious Rockwall. With plenty of room to spare, it is high time this course got an extreme makeover.

In the meantime, the course enjoys a good overall layout, but there is no mounding in the fairways. Very wide open and extremely flat, only six holes have any elevation change. Greens are playable and easy to score on. Fronts are mostly unprotected by traps and only slightly elevated. The lake view is enjoyable and factors nicely into the back nine.

By far the most important club to bring will be the driver. Prevailing winds off the lake will call for careful club selection or you'll find your ball sleeping with the fishes on the approach shots. Beyond that, we eagerly anticipate renovations.

The Godfather – You can go to the Shores in the spring, during the spawn and catch crappie around the lake or you can play golf. I guess they got the name, 'The Shores', because the golf course borders the beautiful chocolate milk waters of Lake Ray Hubbard. It stays in decent golfing shape, but is rarely spectacular.

Double R – Playing close to the lake, you will get lots of wind. Use the bump and run shot when possible. If you get bored, there's always cart fishing.

Jodella – The majority of the holes on this course are really flat, just like the tires on The Vokster and Double R's golf cart after they get through playing golf. Bring your rod and reel; you're just a cast away.

The Vokster – To achieve excitement here, hit the bar heavy before teeing off. And never, ever let the beer babes pass you by.

The Shores Country Club

	Par	Yardage	Rating	Slope
Gold	72	7114	73.9	125
Blue	72	6764	72.1	122
White	72	6104	69.0	117
Red	72	5255	70.7	114

2600 Champion Drive
Rockwall, Texas 75087
(972) 771-0301

www.TheShoresCountryClub.com

Greens – Bermuda

Cost of Play – Mon-Thurs $$ Fri-Sun $$

Bar/Beverage Cart –

Practice Facility –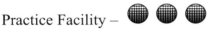

Course Grade –

Overall Grade –

Favorite Hole – Hole #9, 540 Yards, Par 5

Twin Wells Golf Course

Twin Wells is owned by the City of Irving and operated by American Golf. Generally an easy course to play, it is wide open with spacious fairways. Short by today's standards, long hitters will definitely triumph. And on a clear day, there is even a great view of the Dallas skyline from the proshop.

Besides the three holes that snake along the Trinity River and the occasional water hazard, this course offers minimal difficulty. Very little mounding or definition sets the holes apart and any approach shot finding the small greens will be rewarded with a makeable birdie putt.

All the trouble at Twin Wells is clearly visible and the challenge is limited to the pampas grass planted generously around the greens. If your handicap is going up instead of down, come to Twin Wells and watch those numbers fall again. This municipal course is a good value for your dollar, even if what you see is all you are going to get.

The Godfather – Use this course to work out your problems if you are errant off the tee. When your approach shot doesn't find the green, a simple chip shot will leave you with an easy up and down for par. Unless you skank 'em like Jodella does.

Double R – Great ball strikers can go low here. If you are a bogey golfer and shoot in the 90's a lot, playing here is your chance to shoot in the 80's. The biggest obstacle I face here is how to pop the tops on the beer fast enough to keep The Vokster going.

Jodella – A good score can be shot here. With only a few of the par 4's over 400 yards and 2 of the par 5's under 500 yards, birdies should be more common here than seeing The Vokster and Double R with a beer in their hand!

Twin Wells Golf Course

	Par	Yardage	Rating	Slope
Back	72	6636	70.9	117
Middle	72	6213	69.3	113
Forward	72	5056	67.2	113

2000 East Shady Grove Road
Irving, Texas   75060
(972) 438-4340

www.AmericanGolf.com

Greens – Bermuda

Cost of Play – Mon-Thurs $ Fri-Sun $$

Bar/Beverage Cart –

Practice Facility –

Course Grade –

Overall Grade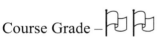

Favorite Hole – Hole #18, 530 Yards, Par 5

WATERVIEW GOLF CLUB

Playing to almost 7200 yards from the tips, the yardage at Waterview could intimidate most golfers. But unlike the other 7000+ yard courses in the Dallas area, the immature trees on this course take the difficulty out of the layout and make the fairways appear wider. With little or no definition to the course, the housing development planned around it is still in the early stages. However, eventually maturity will cause the course to take shape and become a contender among others in its class.

With 6 of the par 4's over 440 yards and all the par 5's playing over 530 yards, it doesn't take a rocket scientist to figure out what to do. Tee it high and let it fly! No worries here. The name may suggest water is a problem, but in fact it is rarely a hazard. Slightly elevated greens will make chipping a bit testy, but with moderate undulation putting will be a pleasure.

Waterview uniquely offers 5 sets of tees enabling any level golfer to compete equally. Play it up or play it back, you can even be a hack, but braggers beware! With wide fairways, very little rough, few hazards and moderate greens, you may not be in the minority.

The Godfather – This is a long golf course that gives you fairways wide enough to land 747's on. Sure, there are a couple of holes that will challenge you, but other than that, just swing away. The fairways are lined with over 1,000 broomstick thick trees. Experienced golfers may not get much out of Waterview, but beginners definitely will. It is a wonderful course for beginners to challenge their game once they graduate from Mesquite Municipal.

Double R – This course sets up well for those of you who are good ball strikers, because there is plenty of room to bang it out there. So if you are spraying the ball a little and having a hard time finding it, then come to Waterview. You won't have any trouble finding it here.

The Vokster – Waterview golf course is definitely built for the silverback gorilla. That's right, Jodella loves long, wide open courses and you will, too. In fact, the hardest thing about this course is bending over and putting the tee in the ground.

Waterview Golf Club

	Par	Yardage	Rating	Slope
Professional	72	7191	74.1	128
Championship	72	6762	71.9	121
Back	72	6355	70.0	118
Middle	72	5906	67.8	110
Forward	72	5472	65.6	106

9509 Waterview Parkway
Rowlett, Texas 75089
(972) 463-8900

www.Waterviewdfw.com

Greens – Bent Grass

Cost of Play – Mon-Thurs $$ Fri-Sun $$

Bar/Beverage Cart –

Practice Facility –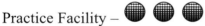

Course Grade –

Overall Grade –

Favorite Hole – Hole #9, 461 Yards, Par 4

Webb Hill Country Club

Webb Hill is located just north of Greenville and was purchased from the United States government by Charles Ranley in the early 1970's. 'A diamond in the rough' is a phrase often used, but seldom true. However, through a lot of sweat and hard labor, Mr. Ranley has brought this diamond to the top of the rough for its 600 plus members and the general public to enjoy.

Playing at 6787 yards from the tips, the course can be as tough as it is beautiful. Large hardwood trees line the fairways throughout providing magnificent beauty complimentary to the elevation so rare in other Dallas area courses. Pause to especially enjoy the Par 5's, there may not be a better combination anywhere else.

Yeah, it is just over an hour from Dallas. But, do yourself a favor and play this track. Just don't tell your buddies, because the good folks at Webb Hill don't like big crowds.

The Godfather – Lulled to sleep? A sweet dream on the first tee box? My sweet dream turned into a nightmare when I was 8 over Par after 5. I've hit more trees here than The Vokster hits the cooler on eighteen holes. Crazy thing is, I can't wait to come back because this nightmare is one I actually enjoyed.

Double R – This course has more ups and downs than Jodella when he forgets to take his medication. So when you play this track, you better hope you have plenty of ups or you will be in for a long afternoon and looking for some medication of your own.

Jodella – The first time I played this course, I didn't think much of it because the first four holes were so easy. Little did I know what was lurking beyond that point. Up and down, around and around, bend and turn. You'd think I'd learn. I finally found a golf course that matches my game.

The Vokster – Get away from the fast paced city life to a truly rural atmosphere. Fresh air, shade trees and a fully loaded cooler may make you pause to spread a blanket, but don't give in. This bad boy is worth the drive all the way to the nineteenth hole.

Webb Hill Country Club

	Par	Yardage	Rating	Slope
Blue	72	6787	72.9	127
White	72	6344	70.6	122
Green	72	5223	69.2	120
Red	72	5441	71.9	123

438 FM 2358
Wolfe City, Texas 75496
(903) 496-2221

no website

Greens – Tiff Eagle

Cost of Play – Mon-Thurs $ Fri-Sun $$

Bar/Beverage Cart –

Practice Facility –

Course Grade –

Overall Grade –

Favorite Hole – Hole #8, 590 Yards, Par 5

Best Overall Top 20

Best Overall Top 20

Criteria: Layout, Challenge, Fun to Play, Customer Service, located in this designated area. If you are only playing 10-20 courses this year, play these.

1. **Cowboys Golf Club** – Best Overall
2. **The Tribute Golf Links** – Best Links Style
3. **Tour 18** – Best 18 Holes
4. **Bear Creek Golf Club** – Best Parkland Style
5. **Indian Creek Golf Club** – Best Municipal Course
6. **Woodbridge Golf Club** – Downright toughest
7. **Lantana Golf Club** – Most Bunkers
8. **Twin Lakes Golf Course** – Best Value
9. **Heritage Ranch Golf and Country Club** – Favorite Par 3
10. **Garden Valley Golf Resort** – Most Beautiful
11. **Chase Oaks Golf Club** – Most Water
12. **The Links At Lands End** – Favorite Lake Course
13. **Tierra Verde Golf Club** – Best Environmental Use
14. **Buffalo Creek Golf Club** – Best Mix of Holes
15. **Tenison Park Golf Course** (Tenison Highlands) – Best Redesign
16. **Pine Dunes Resort and Golf Club** – Best Towering Pines and Sand Combo
17. **The Golf Club At McKinney** – Toughest First Tee Shot
18. **Westridge Golf Course** – 6 par 3's, 6 Par 4's, 6 Par 5's on 18 holes
19. **Bridlewood Golf Club** – Best Subdivision Course
20. **The Golf Club At Castle Hills** – Demanding Par Fours

Top Municipal Courses

Top Municipal Courses

1. **Indian Creek Golf Club**
   (The Creeks Course)

2. **Tierra Verde Golf Club**

3. **Tenison Park Golf Course**
   (Tenison Highlands Course)

4. **Firewheel Golf Park**

5. **Cedar Crest Golf Course**

6. **Country View Golf Club**

7. **Grapevine Golf Course**

8. **Sherrill Park Golf Course**

9. **Stevens Park Golf Course**

10. **Chester W. Ditto Golf Course**

Best/Worst Game
Out Of The Best Overall
Top 20

Best/Worst Game Out Of The Best Overall Top 20

A quick reference for golfers playing from the tips and looking to play or avoid a course based on their strengths/weaknesses. So for instance, if you are a good short iron player, go to Garden Valley for plenty of short iron shots to the green. Conversely, at The Tribute, short iron shots are almost non-existent because of the length.

For the Good Short Iron Player	Your Advantage Is At – Garden Valley Fewer Short Iron Shots Are At – The Tribute/Heritage Ranch
For the Good Long Iron Player	Your Advantage Is At – Twin Lakes/Woodbridge/Castle Hills
For the Bad Slicers/Hookers	Your Advantage Is At – Westridge Expect Higher Scores At – Twin Lakes/Tenison Highlands
For the Hackers	Your Advantage Is At – Tierra Verde Expect Higher Scores At – Chase Oaks
For Good Putters	Your Advantage Is At – Bridlewood Your Toughest Putts Are At – Indian Creek/Golf Club At McKinney
For Straight Hitters	Enjoy Any of the Top 20
For Beginners/Novice	Room To Learn At – Buffalo Creek/Tierra Verde Little Room For Error At – Cowboys/Chase Oaks

For Big Drivers/Bombers	Your Advantage Is At – Tribute/Westridge/Tour 18
For Sand Lovers	Your Advantage Is At – Bridlewood/Lantana/Pine Dunes
Just For Fun	Enjoy - Bear Creek/Tour 18/ Westridge/Links At Lands End
For the Greatest Challenge	Bring Your 'A' Game To – Cowboys Club/Twin Lakes/Indian Creek/Woodbridge

Rankings

Overall Grade

☆☆☆☆☆ – Excellent/Awesome
☆☆☆☆ – Very Good
☆☆☆ – Average
☆☆ – Fair
☆ – Poor

Based on Course, Facility, Bar & Beverage Cart

Bear Creek Golf Club
Bridlewood Golf Club
Cowboys Golf Club
Firewheel Golf Park (New Course)
Garden Valley Golf Resort
Indian Creek Golf Club
Lantana Golf Club
The Golf Club At Castle Hills
The Heritage Ranch Golf and Country Club
The Tribute Golf Links
Tour 18
Woodbridge Golf Club

Buffalo Creek Golf Club
Cedar Crest Golf Course
Chase Oaks Golf Club
Coyote Ridge Golf Club
Grapevine Golf Course
Legacy Ridge Country Club
Ridgeview Ranch Golf Club
Tangle Ridge Golf Club
Tenison Park Golf Course
The Golf Club At McKinney
The Golf Club At Twin Creeks

The Links At Lands Ends
Tierra Verde Golf Club
Twin Lakes Golf Course
Westridge Golf Course

Creekview Golf Club
Firewheel Golf Park (Old Course)
Los Rios Country Club
Old Brickyard Golf Course
Pecan Hollow Golf Course
Pine Dunes Resort And Golf Club
Plantation Golf Club
Prairie Lakes Golf Course
Riverchase Golf Club
Riverside Golf Club
Sherrill Park Golf Course
The Pinnacle Club
The Shores Country Club
Waterview Golf Club
Webb Hill Country Club

Country View Golf Club
Chester W. Ditto Golf Course
Eagle Rock Golf Club
Keeton Park Golf Course
Lake Park Golf Club
L. B. Houston Golf Course
Oak Hollow Golf Course
Stevens Park Golf Course
Twin Wells Golf Course

AAKI Ranch International Golf Course
Lake Arlington Golf Course
Mesquite Golf Course
Red Oak Valley Golf Club

Golf Course Grade

Just the course and nothing else. Based on layout, difficulty, scenery and fun to play

🚩🚩🚩🚩🚩 – Excellent/Awesome

🚩🚩🚩🚩 – Very Good

🚩🚩🚩 – Average

🚩🚩 – Fair

🚩 – Poor

🚩🚩🚩🚩🚩

Bear Creek Golf Club (East Course)
Bear Creek Golf Club (West Course)
Cowboys Golf Club
Garden Valley Golf Club
Indian Creek Golf Club (Creek Course)
Lantana Golf Club
Tenison Park Golf Course (Highlands)
The Heritage Ranch Golf And Country Club
The Tribute Golf Links
Tour 18
Twin Lakes Golf Course
Woodbridge Golf Club

🚩🚩🚩🚩

Bridlewood Golf Club
Buffalo Creek Golf Club
Cedar Crest Golf Course
Chase Oaks Golf Club
Coyote Ridge Golf Club
Firewheel Golf Park (The Bridges)
Grapevine Golf Course
Legacy Ridge Country Club

Pine Dunes Resort And Golf Club
Ridgeview Ranch Golf Club
Tangle Ridge Golf Club
The Golf Club At Castle Hills
The Golf Club At McKinney
The Links At Lands End
The Pinnacle Club
Tierra Verde Golf Club
Webb Hill Country Club
Westridge Golf Course

🚩🚩🚩

Chester W. Ditto Golf Course
Country View Golf Club
Creekview Golf Club
Firewheel Golf Park (Lakes Course)
Firewheel Golf Park (Old Course)
Indian Creek Golf Club (Lake Course)
Los Rios Country Club
Old Brickyard Golf Course
Plantation Golf Club
Prairie Lakes Golf Course
Riverchase Golf Club
Riverside Golf Club
Sherrill Park Golf Course (Number One)
Sherrill Park Golf Course (Number Two)
Stevens Park Golf Course
The Golf Club At Twin Creeks
The Shores Country Club
Waterview Golf Club

🚩🚩

Eagle Rock Golf Club
Keeton Park Golf Course
L. B. Houston Golf Course
Oak Hollow Golf Course
Pecan Hollow Golf Course

Tenison Park Golf Course (Tenison Glen)
Twin Wells Golf Course

⚑

AAKI Ranch International Golf Course
Lake Arlington Golf Course
Lake Park Golf Club
Mesquite Golf Course
Red Oak Valley Golf Club

Fantasy Golf Course

Goofy Golfers Fantasy Golf Course

This is our idea of the perfect 18 holes taken from the courses in the Dallas area. We are talking about the most fun, scenic, and challenging holes you can dream up! In fact, it is our dream to have a helicopter that takes us to these eighteen holes for one truly incredible day of unbelievable golf. Alas, we are stuck with the RV and only an eight hour day. So until someone shows up with a helicopter, we simply have to take solace in knowing that given the opportunity, we have done the work and don't have to waste time making our list.

1st HOLE: Hole #2 – Cowboys Golf Club, Par 4, 376 Yards

You may not realize it, but you are about to be spoiled. What a true rarity for Dallas. The tee box is 80+ feet above the fairway. This is a beautiful hole with a great view, seize the moment to take it all in.

2nd HOLE: Hole #11 – Tour 18, Par 4, 445 Yards

A blind tight tee shot sets up this wonderful Par 4. Duplicated from the #12 hole at Southern Hills, the irony here is how much it opens up once you reach the fairway. Big hitters can hit high draw shots to carry the hill and take advantage of the extra length they can gain going back down the other side. Shorter hitters need to make sure to miss the unforgiving fairway trap on the left. The green is magnificent setting some 30+ feet below you from the fairway. A small water feature with a bridge catches more than its share of short approach shots.

3rd HOLE: Hole #16 – Indian Creek, Creeks Course, Par 5, 601 Yards

This long Par 5 is truly a 3 shot hole even for the longest of hitters. The Trinity River borders the right side from tee to green, forcing golfers to play down the left side among several strategically placed bunkers. The combination will make finding the fairway very important. After two well-placed shots, you will still be faced with a short iron shot that has little room for error.

4th HOLE: Hole #9 – Tour 18, Par 3, 132 Yards

Duplicated from the famous #17 Sawgrass course, this island green claims many balls, especially on windy days. The only out on this teaser shot is the small trap on the front right part of the green. Just because it is short, doesn't make it easy. There is no bail out here! Hit the green or take a penalty.

5th HOLE: Hole #6 – Lantana Golf Club, Par 4, 448 Yards

Pound the driver up the hill here. Miss the fairway traps left or bogey is imminent. Thick trees right give you very little room for error. Once on this very large green, the battle may be won, but the war is not over. Three putts are frequent.

6th HOLE: Hole #5 – Bear Creek Golf Club, East Course, Par 4, 385 Yards

Voted as the #1 Par 4 under 400 yards by The Goofy Golfers, get ready for some fun on this hole. Scattered trees protect the right side and left is a sure penalty. A 230 yard tee shot dead center will still leave you maneuvering your approach shot over two oak trees in the middle of the fairway. Carry your approach shot over the pond to a sloping green for the elusive birdie putt.

7th HOLE: Hole #11 – Twin Lakes Golf Course, Par 3, 214 Yards

You better be hitting the ball well when stepping up to this tee box. A long iron or fairway metal is the club of choice over the lake to the three-tiered green. OB right and green side traps make this one tough shot. Good luck!

8th HOLE: Hole #9 – Westridge, Par 4, 456 Yards

From the tips, this is a very tough tee shot. The tee box and fairway sit at odd angles so lining up is difficult. A large pond resides on the left. The creek on the right actually crosses the fairway and feeds the pond. Get as close as possible to the creek to shorten the approach shot, because this is a long hole. The green is basically unprotected, allowing for a little reprieve.

9th HOLE: Hole #16 – Buffalo Creek Golf Club, Par 5, 551 Yards

Voted by The Goofy Golfers as the hardest Par 5, a lake lies on the left and a small hill on the right makes the drive the most important shot here. That shot will determine how to attack the very difficult second shot. A creek cutting across the fairway forces the players to make a critical decision about whether to lay it up in front of the creek or try to go over it. Words cannot explain just how hard the second shot really is. Finally an easier shot, just don't miss it left in the bunker that is eight feet below the surface of the two-tiered green. Making a par here is a great score.

10th HOLE: Hole #10 – Twin Lakes Golf Course, Par 4, 402 Yards

This Par 4 doglegs slightly right, with a fairway that slopes the opposite direction toward a small grouping of trees. Tall trees and OB on the right make finding the fairway even more difficult. Fortunate players have a mid to short iron into a deep sloping green protected by the lake left and heavy mounding on the right.

11th HOLE: Hole #3 – Cowboys Golf Club, Par 3, 176 Yards

A long but narrow angling green demands proper club selection. Anything short is in the lake that borders the green and anything long finds the big hill behind the green covered in thick rough. Keep your fingers crossed so you don't play to a back left pin.

12th HOLE: Hole #6 – Buffalo Creek Golf Club, Par 4, 478 Yards

What a great, tough Par 4! Usually playing into a prevailing south wind, get all the distance possible off the tee. A pond lines the left side and crosses the fairway, so a conservative tee ball played to the right will make this long hole play even longer. Another pond protects the right side of the approach shot to the green. Par is like birdie here.

13th HOLE: Hole #4 – Ridgeview Ranch Golf Club, Par 4, 347 Yards

Players can hit 5 irons, drivers or anything in between. Watch the creek that swings in on the left side of the fairway, it is farther to carry than meets the eye. Trees down the right side force players to the left. Short irons are hit to a small quick green.

14th HOLE: Hole #10 – Coyote Ridge Golf Club, Par 5, 590 Yards

Get ready. This is one of the longest Par 5's you will every play. Off the tee, there is a lot of room, but watch the OB down the right. Our best advice is to hit as much club as possible on the second shot to land between the two creeks. The left side of the fairway is preferred to give you the best angle onto the green. The green is very elevated and seems to slope from front to back. The only bail out is back right. Good luck getting up and down.

15th HOLE: Hole #16 – Heritage Ranch Golf and Country Club, Par 3, 208 Yards

Voted the best Par three by The Goofy Golfers, this picturesque hole will surely take your breath away. A rock creek runs up the left side and thick trees block the right side. Take an extra club as safety is long.

16th HOLE: Hole #13 – Chase Oaks, Par 4, 387 Yards

Walk up steps and cross the bridge to the elevated back tees. A slight dogleg left through a thick chute of trees makes the tee ball the most important shot here. The left side of the fairway is not an option as you will be blocked by the overhanging trees. An approach shot over a horseshoe bend in the creek requires all carry to a narrow two-tiered green. Long is the only safe bet or kiss your ball goodbye.

17th HOLE: Hole #17 – Twin Creeks Golf Club, Par 4, 413 Yards

Avoid the large pond on the right, but bite off as much as you can chew of the tee shot. A fairway trap left must also be avoided as the hole doglegs right. The approach is not much easier with a large pond on the left side of the elevated green. Missing the green will just about guarantee you a bogey.

18th HOLE: Hole #16 – Chase Oaks, Par 5, 512 Yards

A prevailing south wind in your face adds length to this short Par 5. There are several complications to consider here. Thick trees on the left and a huge rock outcropping in the fairway are very difficult to avoid off the tee. The shots only get tougher. Your second shot will have to avoid OB right and a pond left that snakes in front of the green. The final short iron shot must hit its mark or there is hell to pay.

Frequently Asked Questions

Frequently Asked Questions

Why do you call yourselves The Goofy Golfers?

Jodella: Because we always make goofy comments about each other and our games. We hit as many good shots as bad shots. We would call ourselves the professional golfers, but there are too many of them already.

Why did you write a book?

Jodella: We believe our opinion on the Dallas courses is unique and will be valuable to the average golfer. We thought we could mix information and fun in the same book and I believe we've done just that.

What kind of reaction do you get when people see you in knickers?

The Godfather: Mostly a few questions like where we get them (T. Barry Knickers in California) and why we wear them. Most people like them. And best of all, the really good-looking women ask me for my phone number.

Little Leonard: All positive, we even had a group of ladies at a Tupperware party come out and give us a standing ovation!

What is your favorite type of course?

Double R: The harder the better. We review the beginner courses to do a fair review on them all, but we would rather play the more difficult ones.

Ever thrown a club?

The Godfather: Oh please! Jodella has thrown them, broken them, you name it! We don't call him 'the Great Silverback Gorilla' for nothing!

Tell me about your favorite golfers past or present.

Jodella: Greg Norman. He has an enormous amount of talent and is not a real quiet guy. He has personality and plays aggressive, smart golf.

Double R: Lee Trevino. He grew up playing the same

courses I play. He's a happy go lucky guy and I've never seen him get mad.

The Vokster: Phil Mickelson. He is left-handed and so am I. He has always been right at the cusp of being at the top or near the top and that is kind of how I play in our group. I am not the guy to beat, but I am pretty close to getting there.

The Godfather: I don't have one. I watch the tournaments and realize that my favorite changes from time to time. I enjoy the guys who take advantage of the course and play like I do.

Little Leonard: My favorite is Payne Stewart – no one can touch him. He had the biggest heart and the smoothest swing.

Ever switch partners?

The Vokster: One time I actually switched and tried to play with Jodella and we couldn't even tee off! We tried riding together and Jodella actually got out and walked! So no, we don't do that anymore.

What is the best/worst part of your game?

The Vokster: My driving is good; I don't know what is going on with my iron play.

Double R: My ball striking is consistent, but my putting needs practice.

The Godfather: My mental game is great. I don't have a worst. The rest is all the same.

Jodella: My putting is good, but that can change any day. My driving has always been my worst. People say you play every week, why aren't you better at it? To which I reply, I am better at hitting bad shots!

Little Leonard: My ability to stay close is my best asset. The worst part of my game is my short pitch shots.

What are your favorite area courses?

Double R: My top three are The Links at Waterchase, Woodbridge and Tenison Highlands. They all offer a good challenge for my game.

The Vokster: I enjoy The Tribute, Links at Waterchase and Bear Creek. The Tribute brings back the old tradition and the caddies are a real treat. Bear Creek has been around this area forever and I love their hilly traditional style. The Links at Waterchase has every problem you can fathom and offers a real challenge.

The Godfather: Twin Lakes in Canton is the hardest golf course I have played in this area and really challenges my mental game.

Jodella: My favorites are around San Antonio and Austin, but I do like Sugartree, just west of Fort Worth. I like the taste of hill country flare. I also enjoy East Texas courses because of the trees and dunes. Pine Dunes and Twin Lakes are high on my list.

Little Leonard: I am a real links fan – so I'll take The Links At Lands End and The Links at Waterchase.

What is your favorite club?

Double R: Club Sandwich. Anything with a wedge on it. I have a good feel for the short game.

The Vokster: Canadian Club. My putter, because it is one of the only clubs that I have never taken out of my bag.

Jodella: The ball retriever because it saves me lots of money.

The Godfather: Two iron because I have a good swing with it.

Little Leonard: Any dance club – it's a hobby that ranks right up there with golf.

What's your favorite tournament of the year?

Double R: The Masters and US Open go hand in hand. The Masters because it is the first one and the US Open because it is the toughest. Locally, The Byron Nelson or The Colonial.

In your opinion, narrow it down to the top 5 courses in the metroplex.

The Godfather: Cowboys, Tour 18, Texas Star, The

Tribute and Bear Creek. They are versatile, challenging and awesome places to play. We are spoiled here in the metroplex. It is not uncommon for us to play with people who have to travel hours or even fly to find the caliber of courses we have.

What's on your wish list?

The Vokster: Sponsors! We are always looking for opportunities and ways to promote golf. Visit our website at www.whynotgolf.com. We want to hear from you!

Is there one thing about The Goofy Golfers that the public might not know?

The Vokster: We're just average guys with jobs, mortgages and families. We enjoy each other's company and love the game of golf.

Glossary

The Goofy Golfers Glossary

'A' Game – Your best game.

Adjoining Fairways – Two golf holes running parallel to each other, with little or no trees separating them allowing for errant shots to be found with no penalty and still leaving a shot to your green.

Angling Green – A long narrow green that plays away from you.

Approach Shots – Golf shots that are hit towards the green from the fairway or rough.

A Ringer – A golfer that is brought to play in a tournament because he is an extremely good golfer.

A Shot Maker's Paradise – A golf course that requires a lot of different shaped shots.

Bailout – An area on a hole that allows you to avoid trouble.

Ball Retriever – A tool that extends out to get golf balls out of trouble, also a well-trained dog.

Bean poled – To get a very bad break.

Beer Babes – Good looking beer cart girls.

Beer Sponge – Someone who enjoys a great deal of cold beers.

Big Bombers – Someone who hits the ball a long way (see Bombin' Bettys).

Big Drop Zone – A large area in a fairway or green to hit a golf shot into.

Blind Shot – A shot that is hit to a place where you cannot see the result.

Bogie – One shot over par.

Bombin' Bettys – Anyone who loves to hit the big stick or the driver.

Bump and Run Shot – A short chip shot that rolls toward the hole.

Bunkers – Another word for a sand trap.

Chip Shot – A shot hit by a guy named Chip or a shot made with a very short stroke around the green.

Cool Ones – The Vokster's favorite drink of choice – preferably with alcohol.

Cow Pasture Pool – A slang term for golf.

Divot – The mark a ball makes when it hits the green; also, an indention that is made after a full golf swing. Please repair yours!

Doglegs – The four limbs that keep a dog moving forward; similar to buffalo wings…. A turn in the fairway, not a straight hole.

Drive For Show – When the golfer hits the driver a long way, but still can't score.

Dunes – A large mound of dirt or sand, usually covered with tall or thicker grass.

Eagle – Two strokes under par.

Elbow Room – Room at the bar to drink with both hands. A hole that has plenty of room to hit a shot on.

Errant Shot – Any golf shot hit off line.

Eye Candy – Good looking women, for instance the girls driving the beer cart.

Fairways – The preferred landing area of all golfers. No trouble found here.

Flat As A Pancake – Greens that have very little slope.

Flip Wedge – A soft, floating shot hit with a wedge.

Forced Carries – Whenever your golf cart breaks down and you are forced to decide what to carry; your golf clubs or the beer cooler. Or any stroke that 'forces' you to carry the trouble with that shot.

Fore! – A term used to alert other golfers of your crappy shot just before it whacks them in the head. Apparently just the mention of the word eases the pain.

Four Legged T-Bones – Cattle

Generous Fairways – Wide open fairways with little or no trouble.

Gimme Putt – A putt given to you by your opponent usually no longer than two to three feet.

Goat Ranch – Courses with bad layouts and/or poor conditions.

Golf Etiquette – The proper manners and procedures of playing this hallowed game.

Good Buzz – When twelve or more hornets sting your head or one too many beers.

Great Track – A golf course with a great layout.

Hacker – A golfer that plays golf like he is chopping wood. In other words, not very good.

Hacker Friendly – Easy golf course to play.

Handicapped Holes – Every hole is rated from easiest (18) to hardest (1).

The hardest hole on the course will have the #1 handicap. The #2 will be the second hardest hole on the course, etc. See the scorecards for more information.

High Handicapper – A poor golfer, 100 strokes or worse on 18 holes.

Hightowering Tee Ball – A very high golf shot hit with the driver.

Hook – A ball that travels right to left, struck by a right-handed golfer.

Ice Breaker – Starting off with an extremely tough hole.

Ice Downer – Nobody likes hot beer, unless you're from Europe.

Ka-Thwop Shot – A very, very, badly hit golf shot. Follow us, you are bound to see some.

Let The Big Dog Eat – To hit the driver as hard as you can. Just take it and swing out of your shorts.

Links Style Golf – Golf courses with little or no trees, sand dunes, mounds, pothole bunkers and wind swept grasses.

Little Miscue – When you have struck a shot improperly.

Long Knocking Buddies – More than likely, they are the loud mouth ones of the bunch, always bragging about how far they can hit the ball.

Low-Budget Golfer – Cheaper rates, but don't necessarily expect to play a great course. The upkeep is in direct proportion to the amount of greens fees.

Low Handicapper – A midget golfer (see Little Leonard) or a very good golfer who shoots in the 70's (overall score for 18 holes).

Mulligan – An extra shot with no penalty.

Municipal Courses – A golf course usually more reasonably priced and owned by the city it is located in. Often lacking in maintenance, the good news is they are changing more in Dallas and becoming as distinctive as all the rest.

OB - Out of bounds, not part of the golf course. Results in loss of stroke and distance.

Old Style Golf – Courses with a lot of trees, small greens and shorter in distance.

One Bad Motor Scooter – Evil Knievel's motorcycle and any challenging hole or golf course.

Par – Number of strokes needed to play a given hole.

Par Robber – Anything on the golf course that could cause you to lose strokes.

Par-Robbing Rough – Thick, thick grass. Did we say thick?

Penalty – To have one or more shots added to your score. Jodella usually needs a calculator for this.

Piece Of Cake – Easy golf course.

Pot Hole Bunkers – Small, deep sand traps.

Putt for Dough – Saving strokes and winning money by making a one putt on a green.

Refueling Spot – Any place you can load up with more beer.

Risk/Reward – A shot that is very difficult to pull off, but gives the player the opportunity of saving strokes.

Rough – Thick grass found outside the fairways.

Seasoned Golfer – A person who has been playing golf for a long time.

Semi-Private Club – A golf course that has members along with being open to the public.

Severe Mounding – Any man made mounds along the fairways or a body that hasn't been to Weight Watchers.

Shot Shaping – Having the ability to move the golf ball, while in flight, different directions or drinking shots from different shaped glasses.

Six-16'er – Six tall boys or 6-16 ounce beers.

Six Pack Abs – Opposite of The Vokster's and Jodella's stomach.

Slice – A ball that travels from left to right, struck by a right-handed golfer.

Steep Faced Bunker – A sand trap with a high front to it.

Target Golf – Precise shot making.

Texas Mud Hole – A dried up pond.

Texas Wedge – The only club The Godfather has not broken, the putter.

The Tips – The tee box with the least amount of divots on it. The back tee box where the Goofy Golfers always play from.

Think Style Course – A course where a lot of shots must be thought out and many options are available.

Thirsty Balls – Golf balls that always seem to find the water hazards.

Tricked Up Shots – A hole that demands an out of the ordinary club selection or shot.

Undulating Greens – A lot of slope and mounding making putting more difficult.

Visually Intimidating – A photo of a mad Jodella. Any golf shot that causes concern even before it is hit.

Water Hazards – A creek, a pond, a lake, The Voksters beer, etc.

Wedge – Iron used for shorter distances.

Well Bunkered Greens – Putting greens that are protected by one or more strategically placed sand traps.

Well Struck Shot – A good tequila's not bad. Or a golf ball hit squarely on the face of the club that flies straight, long and true.

Wide Open Holes – Any golf hole that has little to no trouble on it.

Worm Burner – Any golf shot that does not get off the ground.

Jodie, Wes, Luke, Michael, and Riley (The Goofy Golfers) express our sincere appreciation to:
Lynn McWilliams
whose tireless efforts and encouragement made this book a reality.

Lynn McWilliams is a freelance writer specializing in human interest, short stories, public relations, reviews and children's books. She is married to Keith McWilliams and they are the proud parents of Benjamin, 4. Lynn resides with her family in Flower Mound, Texas.

Golf Course Locations

1. AAKI Ranch International Golf Course
2. Bear Creek Golf Club
3. Bridlewood Golf Club
4. Buffalo Creek Golf Club
5. Cedar Crest Golf Course
6. Chase Oaks Golf Club
7. C. W. Ditto Golf Course
8. Country View Golf Club
9. Cowboys Golf Club
10. Coyote Ridge Golf Club
11. Creekview Golf Club
12. Eagle Rock Golf Club (formerly The Summit)
13. Firewheel Golf Park
14. Garden Valley Golf Resort
15. Grapevine Golf Course
16. Indian Creek Golf Club
17. Keeton Park Golf Course
18. Lake Arlington Golf Course
19. Lake Park Golf Club
20. Lantana Golf Club
21. L. B. Houston Park Golf Course
22. Legacy Ridge Golf Course
23. Los Rios Country Club
24. Mesquite Golf Course
25. Oak Hollow Golf Course
26. Old Brickyard Golf Course
27. Pecan Hollow Golf Course
28. Pine Dunes Resort & Golf Club
29. Plantation Golf Club
30. Prairie Lakes Golf Course
31. Red Oak Valley Golf Course
32. Ridgeview Ranch Golf Club
33. Riverchase Golf Club
34. Riverside Golf Club
35. Sherrill Park Golf Course
36. Stevens Park Golf Course
37. Tangle Ridge Golf Club
38. Tenison Park Golf Course
39. The Golf Club at Castle Hills
40. The Golf Club at McKinney
41. The Golf Club of Twin Creeks
42. The Heritage Ranch Golf & Country Club
43. The Links at Lands End
44. The Pinnacle Club
45. The Shores Country Club
46. The Tribute Golf Links
47. Tierra Verde Golf Club
48. Tour 18
49. Twin Lakes Golf Course
50. Twin Wells Golf Course
51. Waterview Golf Club
52. Webb Hill Country Club
53. West Ridge Golf Course
54. Woodbridge Golf Club

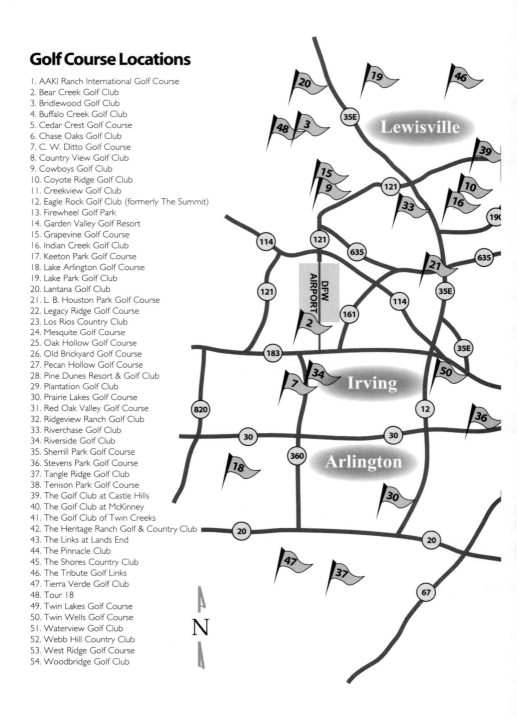

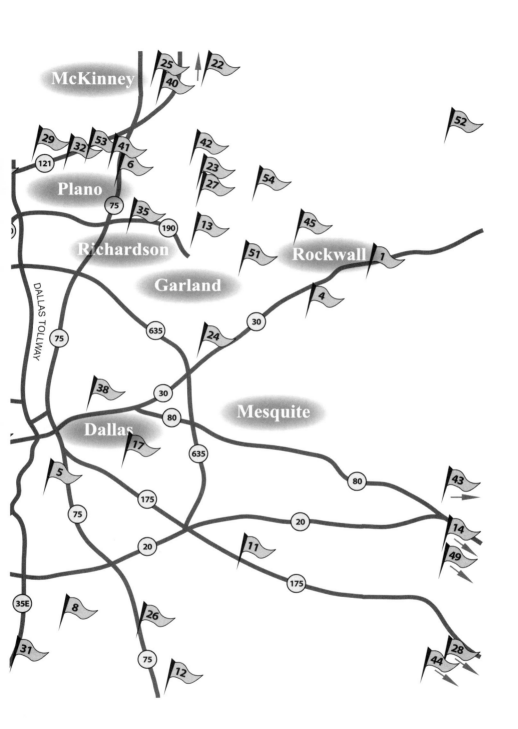